INSIGHT GUIDES

DUBLIN
POCKET GUIDE

www.insightguides.com/Ireland

◉ Walking Eye App

Your Insight Pocket Guide purchase includes a free download of the destination's corresponding eBook. It is available now from the free Walking Eye container app in the App Store and Google Play. Simply download the Walking Eye container app to access the eBook dedicated to your purchased book. The app also features free information on local events taking place and activities you can enjoy during your stay, with the option to book them. In addition, premium content for a wide range of other destinations is available to purchase in-app.

HOW TO DOWNLOAD THE WALKING EYE APP

Available on purchase of this guide only.
1. Visit our website: www.insightguides.com/walkingeye
2. Download the Walking Eye container app to your smartphone (this will give you access to your free eBook and the ability to purchase other products)
3. Select the scanning module in the Walking Eye container app
4. Scan the QR Code on this page – you will be asked to enter a verification word from the book as proof of purchase
5. Download your free eBook* for travel information on the go

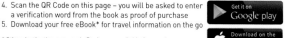

* Other destination apps and eBooks are available for purchase separately or are free with the purchase of the Insight Guide book

TOP 10 ATTRACTIONS

O'CONNELL STREET
Dublin's grand boulevard, studded with monuments and statues, and the iconic General Post Office. See page 62.

KILMAINHAM GAOL
Learn about life behind bars and what brought prisoners here. See page 50.

THE GUINNESS STOREHOUSE TOUR
Find out all about brewing and sample the freshest pint in town. See page 48.

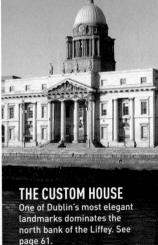

THE CUSTOM HOUSE
One of Dublin's most elegant landmarks dominates the north bank of the Liffey. See page 61.

TRINITY COLLEGE
Dublin's University has a string of famous alumni and owns treasures such as *The Book of Kells*. See page 28.

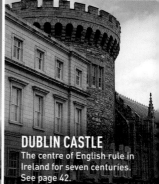

PHOENIX PARK
The biggest urban park in Europe, with landscaped gardens, woods, pastures, various monuments and the zoo. See page 67.

NATIONAL GALLERY
Home to a fine collection of works from the 14th to the 20th century. See page 56.

TEMPLE BAR
A network of narrow cobbled streets with lively bars and interesting markets. See page 40.

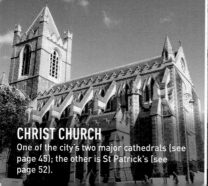

CHRIST CHURCH
One of the city's two major cathedrals (see page 45); the other is St Patrick's (see page 52).

DUBLIN CASTLE
The centre of English rule in Ireland for seven centuries. See page 42.

A PERFECT DAY

8.30am

Breakfast
Make a healthy start at Cornucopia (19 Wicklow Street) and delve into its fresh fruit platters, porridge and muesli, pancakes and homemade hash browns, with lashings of organic tea and coffee.

11.30am

Oriental Café
Walk back up Grafton Street and relax over a coffee at Bewley's, surrounded by the stained-glass windows of the art-deco icon.

12 noon

Exploration
From Trinity, browse the Grafton Street shops as you proceed towards St Stephen's Green. After a stroll on the green, head along the north side, perhaps investigating The Little Museum of Dublin, then passing the celebrated Shelbourne Hotel before exploring the Georgian architecture and fine museums on Merrion Square and Kildare Street. There are plenty of options for lunch in the vicinity: pubs, cafés and fine restaurants.

9.30am

Illuminated manuscript
Turn left out of Cornucopia and cross Grafton Street, to the railings across the road. Follow these left (north) to Trinity College. By arriving here early you should avoid the crowds that flock to see the magnificent library and its illuminated manuscript, *The Book of Kells*.

Major landmarks
At the top of the street is Christ Church Cathedral, well worth a visit along with the adjacent Dublinia interactive exhibition. Then make your way via Christchurch Place and Lord Edward Street for a peek at Dublin Castle.

On the town
Turn left out of the restaurant and take the second left into Eustace Street. This takes you into the heart of Temple Bar where the streets come alive after dark and Irish music fills the air of its legendary traditional pubs.

To the river
From St Stephen's Green take Dawson Street. Turn left at the bottom and veer right back around the front of Trinity College onto Westmoreland Street. At the end turn left to take a stroll along the River Liffey, pausing to glance at the charming Ha'Penny Bridge. Continue and turn left up Winetavern Street just beyond the Civic Offices.

Pit-stop
Cross the road from the castle and go back up the hill. Turn into Cow's Lane with its craft shops and the Queen of Tarts, the perfect pit stop for tea and home-baked treats.

Fine dining
After freshening up at your hotel return to Dame Street and JULES (No. 74 – next door to the Olympia Theatre) for first-class French cuisine in a relaxed, typically Dublin setting.

CONTENTS

INTRODUCTION

Dublin is a fast-paced city, hopping with lively pubs, yet still grounded in its long and literary history. The city has always been on the move, its character infused with both Irish charm and European chic. The amalgamation of old and new, Irish and international, is celebrated in Dublin's spectacular modern buildings, many of them designed and built by world-renowned architects. Daniel Libeskind's Grand Canal Theatre, opened in 2010, is the beating heart of the regenerated Docklands area. In 2009, the Samuel Beckett Bridge, designed by Santiago Calatrava, opened a new route across the city.

At night, Dublin's streets are lively with revellers who pour into the city's pubs, bars, restaurants, clubs and cafés. By day, shoppers throng the popular shopping streets, department stores and shopping centres. The proverbial hospitality and warm welcome have not vanished in Dublin's increasing bustle, though the city's character is more complex than the souvenir shops might suggest.

Dublin sits on 1,000 years of history – and it is present everywhere, from the famous literary homes on Merrion Square to the bullet holes riddling the General Post Office. Yet the city has moved on. It has evolved its own new culture, infused with the international influences of its immigrant communities. Dublin has claimed a seat at the table of cutting-edge European art, design and music. It all merits leaving the pub behind for a while to see what the brave new Ireland is all about.

Beyond the theme bars and displays of lurid green leprechauns and kitsch souvenirs, are the cobbled lanes and galleries of Temple Bar. The works on display show off a clutch of dynamic artists and photographers, whose talent has looked to the world stage. In the boutiques of Grafton Street's Creative Quarter, designers have made high fashion out of hand knits and tweeds, and given home furnishings a new identity. Meanwhile,

Dublin's musicians have long since proven that you no longer need a *bodhrán* (an Irish frame drum) to make it in Irish music.

With renewal comes restoration. The boom years up to 2008 brought with them a new emphasis on historic preservation. Within the city limits you can view artefacts from the Bronze Age, trace the history of the Easter Rising, or revisit Leopold Bloom's odyssey in *Ulysses*. All of Dublin's stories have been packaged and repackaged again, as the destination truly finds its voice once more.

The Samuel Beckett Bridge over the Liffey

CITY ON THE LIFFEY

The River Liffey flows from west to east through the centre of the city to Dublin Bay, forming a natural divide between north and south. Historically, the river has cut a social and economic divide between the middle-class southside and working-class north; the latter often promoted as the only 'real' Dublin. Tactfully the new Docklands development spans both banks of the river.

Further out, both north and south, are the sweeping curves of the Royal and Grand Canals. The occasional cry of gulls and unexpected distant vista, will remind you that Dublin is a city on the sea, and that the Wicklow Mountains hold it close to the coast.

Dublin is a compact city, physically small and tightly packed, making it a perfect place for walking. College Green, the home of

Trinity College, provides a natural focus just south of O'Connell Bridge. O'Connell Street, the city's grand boulevard, leads north to Parnell Square and the Garden of Remembrance. To the southeast is St Stephen's Green, the city's best-preserved Georgian area and the location of the national museums. To the west, along the south bank of the Liffey, is Temple Bar. Uphill from there lie Dublin Castle and Christ Church Cathedral.

ENJOYING DUBLIN

Literature has always flourished in Dublin, the only city to produce three Nobel Prize winning writers – Yeats, Shaw and Beckett. In 2010 Dublin became the world's fourth Unesco City of Literature. Joyce, the high priest of literary Modernism, imagined and interpreted Dublin for the world in *Ulysses*. You will find references to Joyce's work throughout the city.

Dublin theatre is legendary. No visitor should miss seeing a performance at the Abbey or Gate theatres. The city's impact on the rock and pop music scene with the likes of U2 and Bob Geldof is well known – there's even a self-guided tour of their haunts. Traditional Irish music is also alive and well, especially in the pubs, where you might easily walk in on a spontaneous live music 'session'. There has been a modern revival of storytelling, poetry reading and traditional dancing. Visual arts are also finally coming into their own, showcased at the Museum of Modern Art in Kilmainham and and places like the Project Arts Centre on East Essex Street in the heart of Temple Bar.

Lighting conditions

It won't rain on you in Dublin all the time. The climate here can best be described as 'changeable', and yet the sudden shifts from light to dark, sunshine to shower, are part of the city's magic. Buildings seem to transform themselves depending on the light; Dublin under a glowering sky is a very different place from Dublin in the sunshine.

Constantly crowded and busy, Grafton Street is the most chic place to shop, but retailers all over the city carry an international array of goods, as well as Irish crafts and souvenirs. While multinational chains have made inroads, the city is still packed with boutiques and colourful delis. Many shops, hotels and guesthouses have been owned and managed by the same families for years, and theirs is the welcome of traditional Dublin hospitality.

Performing in a Temple Bar pub

CITY AND COUNTRYSIDE

Phoenix Park in the northwest is the largest city park in Europe, and is home to Dublin Zoo. In the centre, squares like St Stephen's Green are the city's small garden oases.

On the coast, Sandymount, Dollymount and Killiney strands (beaches) are the places to go for a blast of sea air (take the DART to get out here). The brooding Wicklow Mountains and National Park provide a more rugged setting, peppered with breathtaking houses and gardens. To the north and west are several historic sites: Malahide Castle, the evocative hill of Tara, and the long barrows of Knowth and Newgrange.

Finally, Dublin is a young city. Thanks to its universities and schools, almost half of Ireland's population is under-25. Visitors on short breaks add to the holiday mood that takes over the city every Friday night and persists into the weekend – and beyond.

A BRIEF HISTORY

Ireland has been inhabited since at least the Mesolithic period, but its history really began with the arrival of the Celts around the 6th century BC. They brought with them iron weapons, chariots and Celtic culture, which quickly gained dominance in the country. This period sparked many myths and legends later romanticised by Irish writers that still exercise their power today.

The Celts were organised into a clan system, and Celtic Ireland became a series of independent kingdoms. These kingdoms acknowledged an elected High King as overlord, with his seat at fabled Tara. There were no towns and livestock was the medium of exchange. Learning was revered, games were played, and the poet was held in awe. Law and religion were important in Celtic culture. The religion was druidic, and the law was an elaborate written code, interpreted by a class of professional lawyers known as *brehons*. The *brehon* laws gave women a high status – they could own property, divorce, and even enter a profession.

CHRISTIANITY AND A MISSION TO EUROPE

St Patrick first came to Ireland as a prisoner, captured in an Irish raid on a Roman settlement in Britain. He eventually escaped, but returned to Ireland as a missionary in AD432. By the time of his death in 465, the whole country had been peacefully Christianised. It was St Patrick who used the example of the shamrock to explain the Christian Trinity to King Laoghaire and an assembled crowd at Tara. The king was converted and the plant has been a symbol of Ireland ever since.

With Christianity and the sophisticated Celtic culture successfully fused, Ireland entered its 'Golden Age' (AD500 until around 800). Ireland's monasteries became major preserves of learning and literacy in the so-called 'Dark

Ages'. Ireland was 'the light of the known world', sending its saints and scholars across Europe as part of the Hiberno-Scottish mission.

THE VIKINGS ARRIVE

Throughout this period, Ireland's political organisation continued much as it had under pagan Celtic rule. There were still no towns; the site of Dublin was only a crossroads, known as *Baile Átha Cliath* ('Town of the Hurdles'). The Irish name is still omnipresent on road signs and buses. From 795, the Vikings repeatedly raided Ireland, sacking the great centres of learning. In the 9th century, the Vikings built a fort on the Liffey and founded Ireland's first town – *Dubh Linn* or 'Black Pool'. The remains of Viking fortifications can be seen today beneath Dublin Castle. The Vikings also introduced coinage and better shipbuilding techniques.

Medieval manuscript made during Ireland's Golden Age

In 988 the Irish kings finally united under the King of Munster, Brian Ború, and drove the Vikings north of the Liffey. After this defeat the Viking influence waned, and they began to be absorbed into the general population. The Irish claimed Dublin and in 1038 the first Christ Church Cathedral was founded.

ENGLISH RULE BEGINS

In 1169 the Anglo-Normans landed in Wexford, beginning the struggle between England and Ireland that was to dominate Irish history until independence. The Norman incursion began with an internal power struggle. The king of Leinster invited Richard de Clare, known as 'Strongbow', to come to Ireland to help him reclaim his kingdom. Successive waves of Anglo-Norman invaders followed Strongbow, bringing with them armour, the use of horses in battle, and the feudal system. Unlike the Irish, they favoured centralised administration, and enforced their rule with the building of fortified castles. In 1171 the English king, Henry II, came to Dublin. He granted a charter in 1174 that gave the city rights to free trade. By 1204 Dublin Castle was the centre of English administrative power in Ireland. The city elected its first mayor in 1229, and a parliament was held for the first time in 1297.

Dublin Castle, a mix of styles from down the ages

BEYOND THE PALE

The Anglo-Normans became rapidly assimilated, following the pattern of earlier invaders. However, the next two centuries were characterised by repeated attempts by the Irish to rid themselves of their overlords. They were very nearly successful: by the end of the 15th century England held only a small area known as 'the Pale' around Norman Dublin. A fortified ditch was constructed in certain areas to protect the now diminutive Norman holdings from the 'wild Irish' controlling the countryside beyond.

All of this changed under the Tudors. Henry VIII and Elizabeth I were determined to subdue Ireland, and launched massive military campaigns. Henry VIII's break with Rome and the Dissolution of the Monasteries meant that by 1558 Dublin's two cathedrals, St Patrick's and Christ Church, had become Protestant (they remain so today). Elizabeth I founded Trinity College in Dublin as a seat of Protestant learning, and it remained just that well into the 20th century.

The Irish continued to resist, but the semi-independent kingdoms were never able to achieve real cohesion. By 1607, they were left leaderless by the 'Flight of the Earls'. Two Ulster earls, O'Neill and O'Donnell, went into exile on the Continent, along with many other Irish lords.

FROM CROMWELL TO THE BOYNE

In 1649, Ireland's most hated conqueror, Oliver Cromwell, arrived in Dublin. His ruthless campaigns resulted in more than 600,000 Irish dead or deported. There was a massive dispossession of the Irish from their fertile lands in the east, and they were driven west of the Shannon. In Cromwell's own turn-of-phrase they could go to 'Hell or Connaught'. Some Irish still spit when they hear his name.

At the end of the century when the Catholic king James II came to the throne, the Irish felt they had no choice but to back him. James was defeated by William of Orange just north of Dublin at the Battle of the Boyne in 1690. As a result, the English parliament enacted the Penal Laws of 1704, which disenfranchised Catholics, keeping the majority of Irish poor and powerless.

GRATTAN AND WOLFE TONE

Wolfe Tone

The 18th century was not a good time for the Irish people, while the political, economic, and social domination of the elite Protestant Ascendancy flourished. Like others before them, Ireland's new leaders had come to identify themselves as Irish, and they were anxious to achieve at least a measure of self-government for Ireland. In 1782 an Irish parliament was formed in Dublin, largely through the energies of Henry Grattan, MP for the city. Grattan succeeded in having most of the Penal Laws repealed. However, the independent parliament was short-lived. Against Grattan's opposition, and through bribery and corruption, it voted to dissolve itself in 1800.

In the meantime, the influential ideas of the French Revolution were spreading. The United Irishmen, led by Wolfe Tone, was founded in 1791, a non-sectarian movement that sought the freedom of the Irish people, both Catholic and Protestant. Wolfe Tone secured aid from France, but a storm scattered the ships of the invading force. Tone was captured and either murdered or committed suicide. He remains a revered figure in the Irish pantheon.

THE UNION AND O'CONNELL

Under the Act of Union, Irish members of parliament now served in London. In 1803 the great Irish hero Robert Emmet led yet another failed rebellion. His speech from the dock and his horrendous execution have become the stuff of legend. Daniel O'Connell carried on the struggle. He formed the peaceful but powerful Catholic Association, and in 1829 the Duke of Wellington, in a bid to avoid a civil war, passed the Catholic Emancipation Bill, which allowed Irish Catholics to sit in the parliament at Westminster for the first time. O'Connell was made Lord Mayor of Dublin in 1841, but failed in his bid to have the Act of Union repealed and an Irish parliament re-established.

FAMINE AND HOME RULE

The Great Famine struck in 1845 with a blight on the potato, the staple food of the poor. It lasted until 1848. It is estimated that more than one million people died and as many emigrated to escape the ravages of the catastrophe. By the end of the 1800s, Ireland's population was virtually halved. There was plenty of food around – corn, cattle, sheep and flour – but it was not available to the poor.

GEORGIAN DUBLIN

The Ascendancy in Dublin enjoyed an elegant lifestyle during this period. Theatre and music flourished. Dublin's importance grew dramatically as the city became the centre of social and business life in Ireland. Craftsmen and architects were imported from Europe and England to create public buildings such as the Custom House and the Four Courts; private mansions like Powerscourt and Leinster House; and Georgian squares like Merrion Square in south Dublin.

The glory of this lively and cosmopolitan city lasted until 1801, when the Act of Union brought Ireland under direct rule from London. Quite suddenly, everything came to a standstill. The rich and powerful left for England, and the city became a provincial capital in a state of long, slow decline.

In America a new organisation formed, the Irish Republican Brotherhood, known as the Fenians. Their rebellion was aborted, but the society remained active and was influential in the efforts of the National Land League, founded in 1879, which sought to change the tenant system. Charles Stewart Parnell, an Irish member of parliament, took up the cause, and the Land Acts, which enabled hard-pressed tenants to buy their land, were passed.

Parnell's other cause was the demand for Home Rule for Ireland. For a time, it looked as if the campaign was going to succeed, but political events, together with the citing of Parnell as co-respondent in a scandalous divorce case, led many to withdraw their support. The bill for Home Rule finally became law just as World War I broke out, but with the proviso that it was not to be enacted until hostilities ended.

THE FIGHT FOR FREEDOM

Two years into the war, on Easter Monday, 24 April 1916, armed nationalists, led by trade unionist James Connolly and poet Padraig Pearse, took control of a number of key buildings in the capital. Pearse read out a Declaration of Independence from the General Post Office (GPO) on O'Connell Street. More than 500 people were killed and many buildings damaged before the Easter Rising was put down. You can still see the bullet holes on the GPO building and the Royal College of Surgeons. Fifteen of the leaders were executed, including Pearse and the wounded Connolly, who was brought to his execution in an ambulance and shot while tied to a chair. The harshness of the British retribution galvanised the Irish and in the words of a Yeats's poem, 'All changed, changed utterly'. People were no longer content with the prospect of Home Rule. They wanted full independence.

In the general election of 1919 an overwhelming number of Sinn Féin ('Ourselves') republicans were returned to

The British send in the tanks during the 1916 Easter Uprising

parliament. Instead of going to London, however, they set up a rebel parliament – the first Dáil Éireann – in Dublin, sparking the War of Independence. This guerrilla conflict lasted until 1921, when a treaty was signed giving independence to all of Ireland, except for the six counties of Northern Ireland where protestant support for the crown was overwhelming. Many republicans baulked at the prospect of only limited independence. Civil war broke out between the supporters of Michael Collins and Arthur Griffith, who had signed the treaty, and Éamon de Valera's followers who disagreed with the partitioning of the country. A year later, the war was over and the new Irish Free State was born.

INDEPENDENCE AND AFTER

In 1937, having made his way back into the Dáil at the head of a new party, de Valera created a republican constitution that took Ireland out of the British Commonwealth. The new republic elected its first president, Douglas Hyde, in 1938.

During World War II, though bombs from German planes fell twice on Dublin, the country remained neutral. In 1948, the Irish Republic severed its last ties to Britain.

Neglect, conquest and isolation, however, had taken their toll, and at first independent Ireland was characterised by continued poverty and emigration, a parochial approach to affairs, and domination by the Church. However, Ireland received huge financial assistance from the European Community, which it joined in 1972, and by the 1990s the economy was starting to boom. The arts began to blossom too, bringing international success to musicians such as U2, Bob Geldof and Sinead O'Connor, while Riverdance transformed international perception of Ireland's traditional music.

In 1990, the dynamic Mary Robinson was chosen as its first woman president, and the Catholic church's influence began to weaken. In 2002, Ireland adopted the euro and the economy boomed, only to crash spectacularly in 2008. In 2011 the long-ruling Fianna Fáil party was resoundingly defeated by a coalition led by centre-right Enda Kenny, and Michael D. Higgins, poet and socialist, was elected president. Reduced wages, increased taxes and mortgage defaulters, many of whom were in negative equity, were among the problems his government faced by 2013. Added to this was the urgent need to legislate for the availability of abortion. The February 2016 election resulted in a minority coalition government between Fine Gael and the Independents with Enda Kenny re-elected as Taoiseach.

The Irish flag flying over the GPO

HISTORICAL LANDMARKS

8000BC First evidence of human habitation in Ireland.

AD432 St Patrick brings Christianity to Ireland.

AD795 The Vikings arrive, building a fort on the Liffey called Dubh Linn.

1014 Brian Ború defeats the Vikings at the Battle of Clontarf.

1038 Christ Church established.

1171 Henry II lands at Dublin and claims feudal lordship.

1204 Anglo-Normans rule from Dublin Castle.

1297 First parliamentary sessions in Dublin.

1534 Henry VIII suppresses Catholic Church.

1592 Founding of Trinity College by Elizabeth I.

1649 Oliver Cromwell invades Ireland and devastates the country.

1690 Supporters of James II defeated at the Battle of the Boyne.

1791 Wolfe Tone's rebellion.

1800 The Irish Parliament is forced to dissolve itself.

1803 Robert Emmet's rebellion and execution.

1829 Daniel O'Connell gets the Catholic Emancipation Act passed.

1845-1848 Ireland's Great Famine.

1916 The Easter Rising.

1919 Sinn Féin forms the first Dáil and declares Irish independence.

1919–21 Ireland at war with Britain.

1922 Outbreak of Irish Civil War.

1927 First general election.

1937 Irish constitution adopted.

1948 The Republic of Ireland Act severs the last links with Britain.

1972 Ireland joins the European Economic Community.

2008 Ireland's economic boom turns into recession.

2011 The government that presided over the boom massively defeated by a coalition led by centre-right Enda Kenny. Michael D. Higgins elected president to general acclaim.

2015 Ireland the first country to legalise same-sex marriage.

2016 New minority government formed between Fine Gael and the Independents.

WHERE TO GO

Dublin is a compact city, and many of its important sites are within easy walking distance of one another. For sights away from the city centre, you can use the bus services or the Luas tram system. You can get information from the Dublin Bus Office in Upper O'Connell Street or from Dublin Tourism (see below). The DART (suburban railway) travels north and south along the coast, making for a pleasant scenic ride. Driving should be avoided, as car rental is quite expensive and the city suffers from traffic congestion and a lack of parking.

Your first port of call should be the **Visit Dublin Centre** (www.visitdublin.com; Mon–Sat 9am–5.30pm, Sun 10.30am–3pm), housed in the former St Andrew's Church in Suffolk Street, or the other office in O'Connell Street. The tourist offices have plenty of maps, leaflets and other useful information. Their bookings service covers accommodation, tours, theatre tickets and entertainment. Dublin Tourism has also devised a series of 'iWalks', which can be downloaded from www.visitdublin.com.

A good way to get the lay of the land is to take the Dublin Bus sightseeing tour. You can catch it from Upper O'Connell Street. Bus Éireann is another sightseeing tour, departing from the Travel Centre at Busáras on Store Street.

The Dublin Pass

Some museums are closed on Monday, and opening hours tend to be restricted during the winter months. The national museums have free admission, but the Dublin Pass, available online and from the tourist offices, gives you free entry or guided tours to over 30 major attractions and museums. Visit www.dublinpass.ie for more information.

The Spire of Dublin, O'Connell Street

AROUND GRAFTON STREET

Grafton Street is Dublin's main shopping street a pedestrianised street jostling with shoppers and enlivened by street entertainers. South of the river, this central pedestrian thoroughfare is lined with stores including the famous Brown Thomas department store, international mostly upmarket brands and Marks and Spencer. The original **Bewley's Oriental Café**, a city landmark for over a century, has been revamped into a popular meeting place with

Grafton Street

its lunchtime café-theatre and front café serving breakfast, lunch and dinner. Stop by to see the café's distinctive Art Deco features, including the rear stained-glass windows by Harry Clarke. On the alley alongside is **St Teresa's Church**, with stained-glass windows by Phyllis Burke and a fine sculpture by John Hogan.

A number of interesting shopping complexes are set around Grafton Street. The smart **Powerscourt Townhouse Centre** is the most notable of these. A signpost points the way just beyond Bewley's to the Clarendon Street entrance. This 1770s mansion was formerly the residence of Viscount Powerscourt and still possesses some magnificent plasterwork. The old house has been tastefully converted, with a pleasant glass-roofed central courtyard surrounded by balconies. There are many cafés and restaurants, and you can shop on the various levels for antiques, crafts and Irish and international designer clothes.

Powerscourt is now the centrepiece of Dublin's Creative Quarter, the epicentre of new Irish design and brimming with fashion boutiques, cafés and bars. The Creative Quarter extends north to Exchequer Street and west via Castle Market (and its chic boutiques and eateries) to bohemian South Great George's Street. The **George's Street Arcade** is a bustling market housed under elegant 18th-century warehouse arches. Retro clothes, street food and trinkets are sold alongside an assortment of cafés and coffee shops. At the other end of the arcade is South Great George's Street, which has more independent shops and the lovely and atmospheric Victorian Long Hall pub, one of the oldest pubs in Dublin.

South Great George's Street leads north to Dame Street. Across the street and to the east is the **Bank of Ireland** (chamber: Mon–Tue and Fri 10am–4pm, Wed 10am–4pm, Thur 10am–5pm). Constructed in 1729 to house the Irish Parliament, the striking building preserves the impressive chamber of the Irish House of Lords with its 18th-century tapestries and coffered ceiling. The building is really a series of additions to an original structure, although the overall effect is one of elegance and superb proportion. The Corinthian portico was designed by James Gandon, who was also responsible for many fine

Powerscourt Townhouse Centre

buildings in Georgian Dublin, including the Custom House on the north bank of the Liffey. Plans to house parliament here after Independence came to nothing; Leinster House in Kildare Street was chosen instead.

Behind the bank in Foster Place is the **National Wax Museum** (www.waxmuseumplus.ie; daily 10am–7pm). Set over four floors, displays cover subjects of Irish history and literature, as well as science and discovery. From the world of media, there is an exhibition on Irish sporting and musical legends. For children there is the Enchanted World and for the brave, a Chamber of Horrors.

TRINITY COLLEGE

Across College Street is **Trinity College** ❶ (www.tcd.ie), founded by Elizabeth I in 1592 to educate the Protestant Anglo-Irish Ascendancy. Only in 1970 did the Catholic Church lift its boycott of the university and proclaim that it was no longer a mortal sin for a Catholic to attend. Today the college is one of the geographic and social hubs of the city, attracting students from around the world. Famous graduates include Jonathan Swift, Oliver Goldsmith, Bram Stoker, Oscar Wilde and Samuel Beckett; resistance heroes Robert Emmet and Wolfe Tone also studied here.

The university sits on College Green, an island of magnificent buildings, open squares and green spaces, surrounded by a sea of traffic. Walk through the gates of the west front, designed by Theodore Jacobsen and built in 1752. The statues on either side are of Edmund Burke and Oliver Goldsmith. You are welcome to explore the campus, but some of the buildings may be closed, depending on the time of year. A good way to do this is to join one of the student-led **walking tours** around the campus, where you will learn about the history of the college and the buildings, and hear some amusing anecdotes about its most famous graduates. The tours run from mid-April until end of September and leave from a desk at the Front Arch (June–Sept daily, every 30-40 minutes from 9.45am; Oct–May Fri–Mon, times vary).

Front Square and **Parliament Square** are 18th century, surrounded by the Chapel, Dining Hall, Examination Hall and 1937 Reading Room, and anchored by the splendid Campanile. On your left, the **Dining Hall** has been falling down ever since it was finished in the 1740s and has undergone frequent rebuilding. Designed by Richard Castle, it was beautifully restored after a damaging fire in 1984. The late 18th-century **Chapel** displays some fine plasterwork and dazzling stained-glass windows, together with a 20th-century organ in an 18th-century case.

The imposing Campanile at Trinity College

Opposite the Chapel is the **Examination Hall**, where concerts are sometimes held; otherwise it is rarely open to the public (look through the spy hole in the door). The beautiful stucco ceiling is by Michael Stapleton, who is also responsible for the ceilings in the Dublin Writers Museum (see page 66). Among the paintings is a portrait of Archbishop James Usher, who donated *The Book of Kells* (see page 30) to the University Library. Both the Chapel and

Examination Hall were designed by Sir William Chambers, the architect responsible for Casino Marino (see page 78).

Built in 1853 by Sir Charles Lanyon, the 30m (100ft) high **Campanile** houses the university's bells. It is impossible to miss the huge *Reclining Connected Forms* by Henry Moore in **Library Square**, or Alexander Calder's *Cactus* behind the Old Library in **Fellows Square**. Architect Paul Koralek's 1967 **Berkeley Library**, fronted by Arnaldo Pomodoro's *Sphere Within Sphere*, fits seamlessly into the earlier buildings. The eastern side of the square once housed Oliver Goldsmith's rooms; renovated in Victorian times, little of the original building remains.

Trinity's most important possession is the 9th-century **Book of Kells**. This ornate text contains the four Gospels and is said to be the finest illustrated medieval manuscript in the world. The exhibition, 'Turning Darkness into Light' (Mon–Sat 9am–5pm; Sun Oct–Apr noon–4.30pm, May–Sept 9am–4.30pm), is in the **Colonnades** beneath the Old Library. It begins with a series of panels explaining how such medieval works were created. The book itself is displayed along with other illuminated manuscripts such as the Book of Durrow or the Book of Armagh. Their pages are turned every six weeks. The exhibition is tremendously popular, so be prepared for long queues at the entrance.

All-in ticket

The Book of Kells admission ticket also includes entry to the Long Room and other library exhibitions. Entry tickets can be purchased at a reduced rate if bought in conjunction with a student-led guided tour of the campus (see page 28).

Upstairs is the impressive **Long Room** (June–Sept Mon–Sat 9am–6pm, Sun 9.30am–6pm, Oct–May Mon–Sat 9.30am–5pm, Sun noon–4.30pm; www.tcd.ie), or Old Library, which opened in 1732. A barrel-ceilinged chamber 64m (209ft) long, with windows

Trinity College Old Library

along both sides, it holds Trinity's oldest books, including a Shakespeare folio.

Across Fellows' Square in the modern Arts Building is the airy **Douglas Hyde Gallery** (www.douglashydegallery.com; Mon–Fri 11am–6pm, Thur until 7pm, Sat 11am–4.45pm; free), a modern two-level exhibition space and the place to go for cutting edge Irish and international art. Alternatively, at the Pearse Street entrance is the child-friendly Science Gallery (https://dublin.sciencegallery.com) – opening hours and exhibitions vary; free.

The Samuel Beckett Theatre and the Players Theatre give budding students a stage on which to shine. Both are located in the **Samuel Beckett Centre** (www.tcd.ie/drama) and produce an array of student productions, with the occasional touring show.

If you'd like to see college life in action – and the weather's good – make your way to the **Pavilion Bar** on College Park, at the opposite end of campus to the main gates. The bar serves student-priced drinks and is surrounded by green spaces that sprout many a sunning student on a warm day. It is a great

Leinster House, seat of Ireland's Parliament

place to relax, watch the rugby team practice and hear others fret over upcoming exams. If the weather's cold, try the **Buttery** under the Dining Hall building – an eatery and bar in the basement that's low on comfort, but full of high jinks.

DAWSON AND KILDARE STREETS

From College Green head through Nassau Street and its craft and souvenir shops, then turn right onto Dawson Street. Here you will find bookshops, boutiques and another shopping complex, the **Royal Hibernian Way**.

St Anne's Church (facing Anne Street South) has some colourful stained glass, and is a popular venue for daytime concerts. A few doors down is the charming **Mansion House**, the mayor of Dublin's residence since 1715. The house was built in 1710 for a property speculator, one Joshua Dawson, after whom the street was named. Behind it is the **Round Room**, where in 1919 the Irish parliament adopted the Declaration of Independence.

Turn down Molesworth Street, lined with several fine-art galleries, to reach Kildare Street. You will see the elegant entrance to **Leinster House**, once owned by the earls of Kildare, and now home to the Irish parliament. This building may have been the basis for the White House in Washington DC, which was designed by Irish architect James Hoban in 1870. Leinster House is open to the public when parliament is not sitting.

On one side of the building is the **National Library** (www. nli.ie), on the other is a branch of the National Museum (see below); 'twin' buildings, each featuring a large rotunda at its core. Tickets are required for the library reading room, which is in the rotunda itself, and worth a quick look without a reader's ticket (available at the information desk). Over half a million items here provide a vast archive of the nation. Exhibitions are held in the splendid entrance hall and a dedicated basement space. The National Library also houses the busy **Genealogy Advisory Service**, which helps those with some initial documentation to trace their family roots. Within the National Library is the excellent Café Joly (www.nli.ie), a perfect spot to relax after visiting the library or the museums of this district. The café serves Fair Trade and organic food.

On Kildare Street, the Museum of Archaeology and History is just one of four branches belonging to the **National Museum ❷**, Dublin's most important historic collection. The other branches include the nearby Museum of Natural History; Collins Barracks near Phoenix Park, and the Museum of Country Life in Castlebar, County Mayo. All are free, all are closed on Mondays, and all share the museum's website (www.museum.ie).

The **Museum of Archaeology and History** (Tue–Sat 10am–5pm, Sun 2–5pm, closed Mon; guided tours take 45 minutes and depart regularly) contains Bronze-Age Irish gold and other archaeological finds. Opened in 1890, the building itself is noteworthy for its entrance hall and Rotunda, mosaic floors

Bust of James Joyce at St Stephen's Green

and the elaborate blue-and-yellow majolica decoration on the pediments and jambs of the doors. The exhibits are state-of-the-art. **Ór: Ireland's Gold** displays the astonishing accomplishments of gold-smiths from 2000 to 700BC. Medieval treasures include the famous Ardagh Chalice and Tara Brooch, along with met-alwork from the Viking period. The museum also has a small Egyptian gallery and an exhibit focusing on the history of Irish independence. There is also a good, but crowded café and a small gift shop.

Deane & Woodward, the architects responsible for the library and museum, also built the Kildare Street Club, in 1861. This marvellous Victorian-Gothic building is famous for the fanciful stone carvings around the base of its pillars. One pillar, reputedly depicting the club members, shows monkeys playing billiards. The club itself was a bastion of Ascendancy establishment. The building (2–3 Kildare Street), now part of the National Library, has a small exhibition area displaying part of the library's vast collection. Here too is the office of Ireland's Chief Herald. The office does not undertake genea-logical research for visitors, but if you qualify and have the requisite cash to spare, you can apply for a Grant of Arms.

ST STEPHEN'S GREEN

Walk to the bottom of Kildare Street and you will reach **St Stephen's Green ❸**, a 9-hectare (22-acre) park in the heart of the city, surrounded by some beautiful buildings. It is the oldest green in Dublin, dating back to medieval times, although only formally laid out as a public park in 1877–80. A popular and often crowded place, the Green contains large formal lawns with ornate gardens, duck ponds, a bandstand and a children's playground.

Entering the park from St Stephen's Green North you will come across the **Wolfe Tone Memorial** opposite the famous Shelbourne Hotel (1824), and behind it a work entitled *Famine*, both by sculptor Edward Delaney. The ***Three Fates*** fountain is a monument to the Irish spirit. Presented by Germany in thanks to the Irish who opened their country to orphaned German children after World War II, the three forlorn figures face Earlsfort Terrace, twisting a piece of string representing fate. Facing St Stephen's Green South is Marjorie Fitzgibbon's

FINDING YOUR ANCESTORS

If you have an Irish last name or Irish ancestry, you may want to join the crowd that comes to Ireland ancestor hunting. Your grandmother's family stories may be the clue – begin at home by collecting family names.

Dublin is a good place to start your search. The National Library on Kildare Street has a genealogical department on the first floor, with a large collection of genealogical and historical records and a free advisory service. Other sources are the Office of the Registrar General in the Custom House, with records of Protestant marriages, births and deaths going back to 1845 and Catholic records from 1861; the Record Office of the Four Courts; and the Registry of the Deeds, on Henrietta Street. If you know the county your family came from, or better still, the town or village, you can go directly to the appropriate parish registers; these go back more than 200 years. Churchyard monuments and gravestones can also be a source of information.

Gardeners tending the Green

bust of **James Joyce**. Working your way around the park, you will see the 1907 **Fusilier's Arch** at the Grafton Street corner.

Leave the park through the arch. On your right are the departure point for horse and carriage tours, the Viking Splash Tour and a stop for the Hop-on Hop-off bus tour. Cross the road to visit **The Little Museum** (www.littlemuseum.ie; daily 9.30am–5pm, 8pm Thurs), which occupies three storeys of a Georgian house. Set up by Dubliners to introduce their city, it offers a fascinating insight into the everyday life of Dubliners over the years. The ground floor hosts temporary exhibitions on Dublin themes, while the first floor front is furnished as a typical mid-20th century drawing room. For many visitors this is the nearest thing to being invited into someone's home. The other rooms of the three-storey house display numerous artefacts, ranging from a vintage telephone and old tram seats to a signed U2 album and a facsimile of James Joyce's death mask. All of the objects were donated by Dubliners to help visitors gain an insight into their city. The curator's tour at 7pm on Thursdays is highly entertaining, rich in Dublin wit and high-grade gossip. At other hours there is usually a knowledgeable guide to talk you around the exhibits. The basement café serves traditional Irish fare.

At the south end of Grafton Street is the **St Stephen's Green Shopping Centre**. A pseudo-Victorian iron-and-glass structure, it was built in the 1980s and is known locally as 'The Wedding Cake'. The centre houses a wide selection of shops as well as a café-restaurant on the top floor, under the glass dome.

Halfway down the west side of the green is the massive Georgian **Royal College of Surgeons**, built in 1806. Those chips in the stonework are bullet holes from the 1916 Easter Rising; the building was occupied by independence fighters led by Countess Markievicz.

One of Dublin's best-kept secrets is the **Iveagh Gardens**, accessible from Clonmel Street via Harcourt Street or from behind the National Concert Hall off Earlsfort Terrace. Neither entrance is obvious, hence the gardens' sense of seclusion. Designed as a series of pleasure gardens in the Italianate style in 1863 – with cascades, spectacular fountains, and rustic grottoes – nowadays it is once again open to the public. Constructed in 1775, the Georgian curve of Harcourt Street was once home to George Bernard Shaw (Nos 60–61, no longer open to the public). A plaque written by the great man himself marks the modest Victorian house where he spent his early years, before relocating to London. From here it is a short walk, following the signs, to the small **Irish-Jewish Museum** (www.jewishmuseum.ie; May–Sept Sun–Thur, 11am–3.30pm, Oct Sun 10.30am–3pm, Mon–Wed 11am–3pm; Nov–Apr Sun only 11am–3pm; free) in Walworth Road. This former synagogue tells the story of the Jews in Ireland by means of documents, memorabilia and old photographs. Set in the heart of what was the city's Jewish quarter in the late 19th/early 20th century, it reveals a little-known part of Dublin's community. Look for a Guinness bottle with a Hebrew label.

Back along the south side of St Stephen's Green begins a fine array of buildings. The first of these is the **University Church**, built in 1853 by Cardinal Henry Newman, then rector of University College Dublin (UCD). The strangely compelling Byzantine-style interior is a very popular venue for weddings. Next door, Nos 85 and 86 comprise the exquisite **Newman House ❹**, part of University College (www.ucd.ie; guided tours June–Aug Tue–Fri at 2, 3 and 4pm). Number 85 dates from 1740 and contains the famous Apollo Room, which has panels depicting Apollo and the muses; and the magnificent rococo salon. Both are by the La Francini brothers, who also worked on Russborough House (see page 75). Number 86 next door, which is largely the work of Robert West, has even more elaborate ornamentation.

James Joyce was a student at Trinity College, while the poet Gerard Manley Hopkins lectured here, towards the end of his life. One of the classrooms Joyce attended can be seen on the guided tour, and Hopkins's room has been restored. The Physics Theatre where Joyce studied overlooks Iveagh Gardens to the rear of the house. Newman House is also used as a venue for dinners, presentations and cocktail receptions.

Just beyond Newman House is **Iveagh House**, home to the Irish government's Department of Foreign Affairs, but closed to the public. Richard Castle designed both Newman House and Iveagh House.

Beyond Iveagh House in Earlsfort Terrace (turn south) is the **National Concert Hall**, of impressive proportions and uncertain acoustics – it is a conversion of an old Examination Hall of University College.

Newman House contains rococo busts of man and beast

Back at the northeast corner of St Stephen's Green, near the Shelbourne Hotel, you can turn right onto Merrion Row to peer through the railings at the small **Huguenot Cemetery** (no entry to visitors). The cemetery dates back to 1693 when French Protestants fleeing persecution in their native land settled in Dublin. They brought with them their architectural and weaving skills, which greatly enriched their adopted city.

At the end of Ely Place, which runs south from Merrion Row and Baggot Street, is the **Royal Hibernian Academy** (www. rhagallery.ie; Mon–Tue, Thu–Sat 11am–5pm, Wed 11am–8pm, Sun noon–5pm; free), where temporary contemporary art shows are held.

OLD DUBLIN

West of O'Connell Street, around Christ Church Cathedral, is the site of the original town of *Dubh Linn*. The founding Viking settlement developed eastwards along the river towards

Trinity College. In 1592, when Trinity was built, the university was not in, but near Dublin.

TEMPLE BAR

Between the river and Dame Street is **Temple Bar ❺**, once a run-down area but now a firm tourism fixture, famous for its nightlife and streetlife. The narrow, partly-pedestrianised, 18th-century cobbled lanes feature some original architecture. The core of Temple Bar can be found in the area between the Central Bank and Merchant's Arch. The area now consists of government-funded arts centres and tourist-oriented shops, with some lively restaurants and bars. The design-led crafts and workshops that originally gave the area its vibrant character have moved east across Parliament Street, and can be found in the Cow's Lane area between Dublin Castle and Essex Quay. Check it out on a Saturday morning when there is a thriving street market for food, books and designer goods.

You can enter Temple Bar from Dame Street, or from Fleet Street (off Westmoreland Street), or you can walk through **Merchants Arch** , opposite the picturesque arching Ha'penny Bridge, into Temple Bar Square. Continuing along Temple Bar, you will come to Eustace Street and Meeting House Square. Most of the cultural centres that make Temple Bar interesting are located in this area. The **Irish Film Institute Ⓐ** (www.irishfilm.ie) in Eustace Street is the main outlet for arthouse and foreign films. It maintains a popular café/bar and its shop has a good selection of posters and books on film theory. Also in Eustace Street is an information office and a cultural centre for children, **The Ark Ⓑ** (see page 98).

On Meeting House Square is the **Gallery of Photography Ⓒ** (www.galleryofphotography.ie; Tue–Sat 11am–6pm, Sun

1–6pm; free), displaying photographs of Dublin past and present alongside changing exhibitions of Irish and international photography. There are also books and posters for sale. The **National Photographic Archive**  (www.nli.ie; Mon–Fri 10am–5pm, Sat 10am–2pm, exhibition area only; free) also located on Meeting House Square, maintains the photographic collections of the National Library of Ireland. There are reading rooms for research and temporary exhibitions.

The **Project Arts Centre** (39 East Essex Street; www.project artscentre.ie) displays avant-garde painting and sculpture and also has a theatre upstairs. **The Button Factory:** nightclub and concert venue is also in the area as well as **Jam Art Factory** Irish art and design shop and **The Ark**, an arts and entertainment centre for children.

On Dame Street, Temple Bar's southern boundary, is a gem of Victorian architecture: the **Olympia Theatre ⓔ**.

At the heart of Temple Bar

Built in 1870, its canopy of stained glass and cast iron is the oldest in Dublin; its enthusiastic interior decoration is also typical of the era. The restored theatre has a regular schedule of light hearted plays and concerts. Just across the way is **City Hall**, originally built as the Royal Exchange in 1769–79. Thomas Cooley designed this fine building's Corinthian portico. The **Story of the Capital** (www. dublincity.ie; Mon–Sat 10am–5.15pm, Sun 2–5pm; group guided tours of City Hall also available) traces the history of Dublin over the last 1,000 years. Just to the west of City Hall lies one of Dublin's most important historic sites, Dublin Castle.

Taking a break outside Dublin Castle

DUBLIN CASTLE

Today, as you walk through the Great Gate into the spacious Georgian yard, **Dublin Castle ❻** (www.dublincastle. ie; guided tours Mon–Sat 10am–4.45pm, Sun noon–4.45pm) looks both serene and imposing. For seven centuries the castle was the real and symbolic centre of British military and social power; it still has resonance for Dubliners today. The castle has been built and rebuilt several times over the course of its history, and little remains of the original Anglo-Norman structure that was built in 1204. It sits on the site of the *Dubh Linn* (Black Pool) that gave Dublin its name.

The guided tour commences with the **State Apartments** on the south side of the building. Lavishly furnished and decorated, with much original period furniture, the rooms are used for ceremonial events, visits from foreign dignitaries, and EU meetings. The **Connolly Room** is so called because it was here that the wounded James Connolly spent his

Castle sculpture

last night before being executed for his part in the Easter Rising. Note the exquisite 'Hibernia Ceiling' in the **Granard Room**; it was moved here from Mespil House. The **Drawing Room** was partially destroyed by fire in 1941, so its furnishings are faithful reproductions; the huge (repaired) Ming punch bowl is particularly striking.

A splendid carpet, with a design based on a page from the Book of Kells (see page 30), covers the floor of the **Throne Room**. In 1911, George V was the last to use the rather large throne. In the lovely **Picture Gallery**, convex wall mirrors made it possible for the host at table to keep his eye on everyone, particularly the servants. The enormous **St Patrick's Hall**, with its painted ceiling by Vincenzo Valdre, contains the banners and coats of arms of the now-defunct Knights of St Patrick. The hall is now used for the inauguration of the Irish president.

One of the most interesting parts of the tour is the excavation of the **Viking and Norman Defences**. Visitors can stand in the dry bed of the old moat, traverse imaginative gangways over the encroaching river (the Poddle, not the Liffey), and view the stairs at which boats once landed provisions for the castle. In the restored **Treasury** (built in 1715, located in the Lower Yard), browse in the bookshop or relax in the Vaults Restaurant.

The oldest part of the castle is the **Record Tower** (1258), which contains the Garda (Police) museum, visible as you leave the upper yard. The neo-Gothic **Church of the Most Holy Trinity**, adjacent to the tower, has stone work by Edward Smyth and a fan-vaulted ceiling. The Crypt Theatre is under the church and presents exhibitions, plays and concerts.

A modern addition to the castle precinct is the award-winning **Chester Beatty Library** ❼ (www.cbl.ie; May–Sept Mon–Fri 10am–5pm, Sat 11am–5pm, Sun 1–5pm, Oct–Apr closed Mon; free), which moved here from Ballsbridge. The library is a treasure house of Islamic manuscripts, Chinese, Japanese and Indian art and texts. Biblical papyri and Christian manuscripts are also on display, completing one of the richest collections of the written word in Western and Eastern cultures. The library itself includes copies of the Koran and codices dating from the second century BC. The gallery's marvellous Silk Road Café provides a menu to match the cultures of the displays.

THE LEGEND OF BRITISH JUSTICE

Above the main gate of Dublin Castle stands a statue of Justice. With its back turned to the city, it was an apt symbol of British rule. The farce does not end there. This Justice, thanks to the naivety of the sculptor, has no blindfold. Furthermore the statue, inadvertently of course, drained rainwater from the head, down the arm and into the metal scales she holds, tipping them out of balance.

Christ Church Cathedral

CHRIST CHURCH CATHEDRAL AND ENVIRONS

Further up the hill on Castle Street from the Great Gate is the first of Dublin's two major cathedrals, **Christ Church Cathedral** ❽ in Christchurch Place (www.christchurchdublin.ie; Mon–Sat from 9am; Sun from 12.30-2:30pm). Like the castle, the cathedral stands on a hill, rising on the site of King Sitric's 11th-century wooden church. The foundations date back to 1172 when Strongbow, the Earl of Pembroke, had it rebuilt as a stone structure. By 1558, after Henry VIII's break with the Roman Catholic Church, all the existing foundations in Dublin had become Anglican.

Unfortunately, the church building was massively and unsympathetically restored in 1871–8, when most of the original interior was ripped out. However, there is still much to appreciate in Christ Church, including the impressive stonework, soaring nave, and the handsome 19th-century encaustic floor tiles based on a 13th-century pattern. Strongbow's tomb is in the church; while in the **Peace Chapel** is a somewhat macabre

Welcome to Dublinia!

artefact. The embalmed heart of St Laurence O'Toole, the influential 12th-century archbishop of Dublin, is kept in a cage suspended on the wall near the altar. The cathedral choir traces its origins back to 1480 and has the distinction of taking part in the world's first ever performance of Handel's *Messiah*. Choral Evensong is on Sundays, Tuesdays, Wednesdays and Thursdays at 6pm.

The vast, vaulted medieval crypt is the oldest structure in Dublin. An exhibition, entitled **Treasures of Christ Church**, takes up much of the crypt. An additional charge is required to see this limited number of ancient texts, plus the tabernacle of James II, a William of Orange plate, commemorating his victory in the Battle of the Boyne, and a 1666 Common Prayer Book. A few items of note are in the open areas of the crypt, among the forest of heavy stone pillars. These include stocks dating from 1670, medieval carved stones and a curious exhibit–a mummified cat and a rat, found trapped in the organ pipes.

In the Old Synod Hall, just across the road from the cathedral (and linked to it by a bridge), you will find **Dublinia and the Viking World ❾** (www.dublinia.ie; daily March to Sept 10.00am-6.30pm, Oct to Feb 10am-5.30pm). This impressive re-creation of Dublin in medieval times incorporates state-of-the-art interactive exhibits and reconstructions to enhance the sights, sounds and even the smells of the city of the period. Exhibitions include an archaeological lab and excavation site, life on board a Viking warship, burial customs and the looting of monasteries. You can also climb St Michael's Tower for a view over the city.

Wood Quay, on the south bank of the river is the site of the original Viking settlement. It stands downhill from the arch and is dominated by the offices of the Dublin Corporation. The construction of these offices obliterated much of the archaeological dig that unearthed the original layout of the 9th-century quay, but the artefacts that were found are on view in the National Museum (see page 33).

A short distance from the cathedral on High Street are the two **St Audoen's churches**. The restored Church of Ireland St Audoen's is the older of the two (c.1190) and is the only remaining medieval church in the city (interior access Jun–Oct daily 9.30am–4.45pm). Next door is the narrow, lofty,

Going with the flow at the Guinness Storehouse

neoclassical facade of Catholic St Audoen's, built in 1847. Both churches stand beside what remains of the old city walls, and St Audoen's is the only surviving gate. In medieval times the High Cross of the Norman city, where decrees and notices of excommunication were read out, stood on the High Street. Granite markers erected in 1991 indicate the line of the old city walls.

West from here in Thomas Street, a plaque on the decommissioned and forlorn-looking **St Catherine's Church** (built in 1769) marks the spot where the famed Irish resistance hero Robert Emmet was hanged in 1803. **John's Lane Church** further down Thomas Street is more remarkable. Though just over 100 years old, it is one of the most attractive churches in the city. Thomas Street West becomes James's Street, where the **Guinness Brewery** has been situated ever since 1759.

GUINNESS BREWERY AND BEYOND

Well west of the city centre lie several of Dublin's top tourist attractions. Handily, they are all clustered near Heuston Station, which is well serviced by buses and trams from the centre. The **Guinness Storehouse** ❿ (www.guinness-storehouse.com; daily 9.30am–7 pm, July–Aug until 8 pm) is the latest incarnation of the Guinness Brewery tour and an ultra-modern one at that. This self-guided tour begins on the ground level with ingredients and ends in the very stylish

Enjoying the view of Dublin from the Gravity bar

A tour of Kilmainham Gaol

Gravity Bar atop the brewery with a 360-degree view of Dublin and the freshest (and free-est) pint of Guinness in town. Along the way you get to see and sniff the various stages of the brewing process. Despite all the entertaining technology, the tour is ultimately educational, as you watch films of old coopers making the casks for the brew and learn just how Guinness is created from the four simple ingredients of water, barley, hops and yeast.

The restored Royal Hospital at Kilmainham, which now houses the **Irish Museum of Modern Art** ⓫ (www.imma.ie; Tue–Sat 10am–5.30pm, Wed from 10.30am, Sun noon–5.30pm, closed Mon; free) is Dublin's most important 17th-century building (1684). With its wonderful light and space, it makes a tremendous exhibition area. The museum's holdings include the Gordon Lambert Collection, with more than 100 works dating from the 1960s–70s. However, the real attractions are the numerous temporary exhibits. There is an international residency programme for artists, and visitors may meet the artists in their studios (depending on schedules). Concerts and special events are also held in the museum, and there is an atmospheric café in the vaults. A good range of contemporary art books, posters and postcards can be found in the gallery bookshop.

The former Collins Barracks – now a museum

Further west is the evocative museum of the **Kilmainham Gaol ⑫** (www.heritageireland.ie; Apr–Sept daily 9.30am–6pm, Oct–Mar Mon–Sat 9.30am–5.30pm, Sun 10am–6pm). Kilmainham was the major Irish prison for well over a century, with Éamon de Valera as its last prisoner in 1924. An excellent exhibition traces the history of the prison, as well as the political and social events that brought many of the prisoners here. Victorian theories about prisons and the treatment of prisoners are explored in one exhibition space. A 25-minute audio-visual presentation in the prison chapel is followed by a guided tour through the dark corridors of the 18th-century part of the building, where you can see the cells occupied by the condemned leaders of the Easter Rising – they were executed in the prison yard.

Nearby, on the south bank of the Liffey opposite Phoenix Park, is the **Irish National War Memorial Park.** Created in the 1930s to designs by the architect and landscape designer Edwin Lutyens, the gardens are a tribute to the thousands of Irish soldiers who died in World War I while serving in the British Army. The sombre design incorporates the War Stone and four granite pavilions, one of which contains Celtic and art deco illuminated manuscripts by the book illustrator Harry Clarke, listing the names of those killed in action.

On the north bank of the Liffey, behind Wolfe Tone Quay, are the former **Collins Barracks**. Built in 1701, the barracks were occupied continuously until 1997. Since then, they have been home to the **National Museum of Decorative Arts and History**  (www.museum.ie; Tue–Sat 10am–5pm, Sun 2–5pm; free). Silver, ceramics, furniture and folk artefacts trace Ireland's social and political history. There is also a café and bookshop.

THE LIBERTIES

Back towards the city centre now, and to the south of High Street, the area known as the **Liberties** was so named because it was situated outside the medieval city walls and was run by local courts, free of city regulations on trade. The area, once impoverished, is slowly gentrifying, with new housing and restoration of the original small red-brick houses.

Across from the two St Audoen's (see page 47), two interesting streets run off High Street. Francis Street is lined with antiques shops, full of glittering treasures. In

St Patrick's Cathedral choir

Back Lane are the headquarters of An Taisce, an organisation dedicated to the preservation of historic buildings and gardens in Ireland. Its home is the delightful **Tailors' Hall**, the oldest guildhall in Ireland, once used by hosier and barber-surgeons' guilds as well as by the tailors. It dates from 1706, and is one of the few remaining original Queen Anne buildings in Dublin.

ST PATRICK'S CATHEDRAL

At the eastern end of Back Lane and turning right, Nicholas Street becomes Patrick Street. On the left, off St Patrick's Close, is **St Patrick's Cathedral** ⓮ (www.stpatrickscathedral.ie; Mar–Oct Mon–Fri 9.30am–5pm, Sat 9am–6pm, Sun 9–10.30am, 12.30–2.30pm, 4.30–6pm; Nov–Feb Mon–Fri 9.30am–5pm, Sat 9am–5pm; Sun 9–10.30am, 12.30–2.30pm (outside service times)). This is the oldest Christian site in Dublin. St Patrick himself is reputed to have baptised converts on this spot, marked by a Celtic cross in the nave, suggesting that there has been a church here since around AD450. In the adjoining St Patrick's Park a marker shows the site of **St Patrick's Well**.

The grave of Jonathan Swift

The height and space of the cathedral are impressive. Note the carved helmets and swords set above the choir stalls and the 19th-century tiled floor, similar to the one in Christ Church. The 90m (300ft) interior makes it the longest church in the country. The 45m (150ft) tower holds the largest ringing peal of bells in Ireland. Not

Typical Georgian doorways on Merrion Square

much is left of the original construction of 1191. Destroyed in a fire in the 14th century, it was later rebuilt, and even includes some Victorian restoration work.

The cathedral has had a varied history. From 1320 until Henry VIII closed it, St Patrick's was the seat of Ireland's first university. Later, Cromwellian troops used the aisles to stable their horses. The great Jonathan Swift, author of Gulliver's Travels, was dean here from 1713 to 1745. He was much revered for his charity and his championship of the Irish cause. You can see his grave and that of his great love, Esther Johnson, as well as the pulpit from which he preached. On the wall is the epitaph he wrote for himself.

An interesting artefact from the medieval chapter house is a door with a hole in it. Lord Kildare cut the hole in 1492 so he could reassure his archenemy Lord Ormonde, who was under siege in the chapter house, of his friendly intentions. Kildare put his arm through the hole, thus giving rise to the common expression 'to chance your arm'.

Also in St Patrick's Close (left from the cathedral exit) is **Marsh's Library** ⓑ (www.marshlibrary.ie; Mon and Wed–Fri 9.30am–5pm, Sat 10am–5pm). The first public library in Ireland was founded in 1701 and held more than 25,000 books, most dating from the 16th to the 18th century. The oak shelving is original, as are the metal cages in which scholars were locked so as to prevent thefts. Even if you are not a scholar, do come here – the atmosphere and beauty of the place is entrancing.

GEORGIAN DUBLIN

Georgian architecture is found all over the city; however, the harmonious streets and squares lying to the southeast of Nassau Street truly deserve the title. In addition to superb buildings, there are several important museums and galleries to visit, and the banks of the Grand Canal provide leafy, shaded walks.

MERRION SQUARE

Clare Street, at the eastern end of Nassau Street, runs into **Merrion Square North**, where you will find some of the area's finest houses. The square dates from 1762; houses here were the homes of high society, including many members of parliament and famous artists and writers. Look for individual details – the painted doors, the fanlights, and the door knockers, some in the form of a fish or a human hand.

On Merrion Square West is the National Gallery of Ireland, which provides tickets for free 40-minute tours of the restored **Government Buildings** (Upper Merrion Street; tours Sat 10.30am–1.30pm on the hour, tickets available from 10am on the morning of the tour from the National Gallery; free). Refurbished in 1990–91 and housing the offices and meeting rooms of the Taoiseach (Prime Minister) and his cabinet, the interior rooms of the buildings are a fascinating and tasteful combination of the old and the new. A magnificent Evie

Government Buildings

Hone stained-glass window adorns the landing in the main entrance; it is beautifully complemented by the carpet and balustrade designed by Mary Fitzgerald. There is some excellent contemporary furniture and a miniature of Oisín Kelly's sculpture The Children of Lir. Outside, the courtyard is paved in limestone tram-setts from the streets of Old Dublin.

Also in Merrion Street, next to the front garden of Leinster House, is the **Natural History Museum** (www.museum.ie; Tue–Sat 10am–5pm, Sun 2pm–5pm; free). This museum opened in 1857 with a speech by Dr Livingstone. Set in a compact neoclassical building, it is a wonderful shrine to the late-Victorian obsession with travelling and collecting. Old and young warm to the displays of stuffed animals and birds in glass cases, with Irish fauna on the ground floor and more exotic creatures including an Indian elephant upstairs. Marvel at the huge antlers of the giant Irish deer who roamed Ireland 10,500 years ago, and whose skeletons were preserved in bogs.

Statue of Oscar Wilde

The **National Gallery of Ireland** ⑯ (Mon–Sat 9.15am–5.30pm, Thu until 8.30pm, Sun 11am–5.30pm; free; www.nationalgallery.ie; the Milltown and Dargan wings are closed for upgrade until 2016) houses a fine collection of works from the 14th to the 20th centuries, from Goya, Brueghel, Titian, Velasquez, Rembrandt and Gainsborough, to Monet, Degas and Picasso. One of the gallery's most important paintings, discovered in the house of the Jesuit Brothers in 1993, is Caravaggio's long-lost masterpiece, *The Taking of Christ*. There is also a fine collection of Irish art, including a whole roomful of Jack Yeats's paintings. There are also water-colours, drawings, prints, sculpture and a multimedia gallery offering information about 100 of the gallery's best works. There is a good bookshop and the spacious Winter Garden café. Ongoing renovations mean that not all of the galleries are open to the public.

Enter one of the many gates of **Merrion Square Park** and walk along some of the secret, wooded paths to the immaculately groomed gardens. Do not miss Danny Osborne's **statue of Oscar Wilde**, wearing a smoking jacket with red lapels and reclining on a rock in the northeast corner of the park. At the height of the Great Famine in 1845–7, a soup kitchen was set up here to feed the starving. You will want to return here to browse the **Boulevard Galleries** of art set up around the square on summer weekends.

FITZWILLIAM SQUARE AND BEYOND

Take the time to stroll down the streets around Merrion Square, which were laid out at the same time. At the eastern end of Upper Mount Street you will notice the distinctive shape of the Greek-revival **St Stephen's Church**, which dates back to 1824. For obvious reasons it is known universally as the 'Pepper Canister Church'. Occasional events and concerts are held here.

Lower Fitzwilliam Street, at the southeast corner of Merrion Square, houses the offices of the Electricity Supply Board. They tried to make up for the ugliness of their new premises by restoring **Number Twenty Nine** ❶ (www.esb.ie/numbertwentynine; Tue–Sat 10am–5pm, Sun noon–5pm) as a museum representing a typical bourgeois house of the period. Indeed, this lovely Georgian townhouse has been superbly fitted out to reflect middle-class life in the late 18th to early 19th century. An audio-visual display, cosily narrated by the 'ghost' of the former owner and her much put-upon maidservant, is followed by a half-hour guided tour for up to ten people. The staff are friendly and helpful, and there is a small tearoom. The place can get very busy, though.

The street crosses Lower Baggot Street and leads on to **Fitzwilliam Square**, which

Picture this...

The star exhibits of the Natural History Museum, a species once known as Irish Elk, megaloceros giganteous, has been renamed Giant Deer. They are neither elk, nor exclusively Irish. Standing over 2m (62.5 ft) tall, with antlers measuring nearly 4m (13ft) across, they flourished across Europe during the last Ice Age some 10,500 years ago. In Ireland the skeletons were preserved in bogs following a rise in sea level, and disinterred in the 19th century.

Crossing Fitzwilliam Square in style

has a park open to residents only. The last Georgian square built in Dublin, it was completed by 1830, although the older houses date back to 1714. Here, as elsewhere in Georgian Dublin, there is exquisite detail in the doorways and fanlights, and the ironwork of the balconies.

Return to Baggot Street, and turn left (SE) to the junction with Herbert Place. Beyond Baggot Street Bridge to the east is the suburb of **Ballsbridge**, at the heart of which are the grounds of the **Royal Dublin Society** (RDS) where the famous Dublin Horse Show takes place.

If you turn right at Baggot Street Bridge along the towpath of the **Grand Canal**, you can see a bronze statue of the Irish poet Patrick Kavanagh, who died in 1967; the poet is shown in relaxed pose, on a bench. The pleasant towpath walk, under a canopy of leaves, goes past the gardens of terraced houses, offices and apartment buildings. There are plenty of ducks, moorhens and swans, and the canal is spanned by the distinctive curves of the 18th-century bridges.

For a total contrast, walk along Herbert Place in the opposite direction and follow the canal to Grand Canal Square, the heart of Dublin's ambitious Docklands Development (www.ddda.ie has a map and more information), and the location of Daniel Libeskind's stunning theatre. In fine weather kayakers ply the water on Grand Canal Dock, while office workers relax over an outdoor coffee from one of the many food outlets. The headquarters of both Google and Facebook are based in this lively new quarter. From here you can cross to the northside of the Liffey on the beautiful Samuel Beckett Bridge, designed by Santiago Calatrava.

NORTH OF THE RIVER

Dublin north of the Liffey has its own atmosphere and, like the southern part of the city, some magnificent buildings, museums, and Dublin's two most important theatres.

ALONG THE QUAYS

Crossing **O'Connell Bridge**, there are fine views along the river. The Custom House is on the right and to the left is the equally splendid Four Courts. The bridge was built in 1790 and widened until it was almost square in 1880. To the north of the river a boardwalk leads to Liffey River Cruises (www.liffeyrivercruises.com; daily, Mar–Oct 11.30, 12.30, 2.15pm, 3.15pm; April and Sept also at 4.15pm, May–Aug also at 10.30am). Take an

Patrick Kavanagh

Patrick Kavanagh was born in 1904 at Mucker, Inniskeen, County Monaghan. His father eked a living from the land and by repairing the shoes that walked upon it. Young Patrick joined in these trades with little success. Local farmers made a joke of his farming skills and called him a fool for pursuing poetry. He moved to Dublin and in 1936 *Tarry Flynn*, his first publication, set his reputation on its way.

hour-long river cruise on an all-weather boat with live historical commentary on some of Dublin's finest buildings.

Turning left along the quays of the north bank towards the Four Courts (about 1.5km/1 mile), you will reach the cast-iron **Ha'penny Bridge**, which connects Merchants' Arch to Liffey Street. The footbridge was built in 1816; its name refers to the toll once levied for crossing. Looking up river, the next bridge is the pedestrian **Millennium Bridge**. On the corner of Liffey Street is a **sculpture** known locally as 'the hags with the bags'. Two doors down from the bridge are the charming Winding Stair bookshop and restaurant.

James Gandon designed the **Four Courts** in 1785. The building is a majestic sight with its Corinthian portico crowned with statues and its columned dome. It holds the various courts of the city. The building was damaged in the fighting of the 1920s and a fire destroyed all the official archives, but thorough restoration work was carried out in 1932. You can step inside when the courts are in session (tel 353 1 888 6000; Mon–Fri 10am–1pm, 2–4pm, but check in advance).

Turn north into Church Street to find **St Michan's Church** ⓲ (Mar–Oct Mon–Fri 10am–12.45pm and 2–4.30pm, Nov–Mar Mon–Fri 12.30–3.30pm, Sat all year 10am–1pm; charge for tours). Built in the 17th century on the site of a Danish chapel, the church's chief claim to fame is its vaults. Thanks to their limestone composition, the vaults preserve bodies buried there in a mummified state. A few of the bodies are on display. Robert Emmet is thought to be buried in the graveyard of the church, and Parnell's funeral service was held here. Handel is said to have practised on the 1724 organ while composing The Messiah.

The **Old Jameson Distillery** ⓳ (daily 9am–6pm, last tour 5.15pm) is in Smithfield, the heart of Old Dublin. If you ever wanted to know more about the fascinating craft of whiskey

The imposing Four Courts

making, this award-winning attraction is the place to find out. Located on the original site of the Jameson Distillery in cobbled Bow Street, it also offers a history of the distillery itself. Behind the building is Smithfield Market, Dublin's fruit, vegetable and flower market. A traditional horse fair is held here on the first Sunday of March and September, the last vestige of a long tradition of inner city horse dealing.

If you turn right instead of left from O'Connell Bridge, you will come to one of Dublin's great architectural masterpieces, the **Custom House** ⓴ (www.visitdublin.com; mid-Mar–Oct, Mon–Fri 10am–12.30pm, Sat–Sun 2–5pm, winter Wed–Fri and Sun only; free). Designed by James Gandon as his first Dublin masterpiece, it was built in 1791. The sculpture on the dome (a personification of Commerce) and the river gods (including Anna Livia, set over the main door) are by Edward Smyth, who was also responsible for the statues on the GPO (see page 62). The north side of the building has statues by Joseph Banks depicting Africa, America, Asia and Europe.

On Custom House Quay is Dublin's **Famine Memorial**. Unveiled in 1998, this is a series of striking life-size bronze figures by sculptor Rowan Gillespie. Their gaunt and emaciated features are given added poignancy by the fact that they appear to be walking past the gleaming facade of the Allied Irish Bank, looking east towards the Irish Sea.

O'CONNELL STREET

O'Connell Street is a grand boulevard with a wide central section, studded with monuments and statues. It runs in a straight line north from O'Connell Bridge, and the best way to view it is to walk down the central island, making excursions to the left and right at the zebra crossings.

The road was largely destroyed in the Rising (see page 20), but was restored by the end of the 1920s. At the foot of the bridge is John Foley's **monument to Daniel O'Connell**, surrounded by four victory figures and peppered with bullet holes from 1922. Oisín Kelly's memorial to working-class hero, orator, and socialist **Jim Larkin** is opposite the famous chiming clock of **Clerys**, one of the world's first purpose-built department stores, founded in 1853. Farther up on the right is one of Dublin's legendary hotels, the Gresham, which was built in 1817, seven years before the Shelbourne.

Famine Memorial

In the centre of O'Connell Street is the **General Post Office** 21 (Mon–Sat 8am–8pm). Built in 1815–18, it is one of the last great buildings to come out of Dublin's Georgian boom, and is renowned for its imposing

Detail of the monument to Daniel O'Connell

Ionic portico (look for the bullet holes) with six fluted columns and figures sculpted by Edward Smyth. It was here, in 1916, that James Connolly and Padraig Pearse barricaded themselves inside and proclaimed the Irish Republic. The post office was virtually destroyed in the fighting but has since been restored. The Rising is commemorated in the main hall by a beautiful bronze statue of the mythic folk hero **Cúchulainn** and by ten paintings illustrating various scenes of the rebellion. There is also the An Post Museum tracing the history of the post office in Ireland.

O'Connell Street has benefited from a renovation programme that created a pedestrian plaza with trees, street furniture and special lighting in front of the GPO. The **Spire of Dublin** ㉒ was erected in 2003 on the old site of Nelson's Pillar. It stands 120m (394ft) high and a time capsule has been sealed beneath it. From the very start it has been popular among Dubliners as a shiny new monument for their much loved but much battered city. Just off Lower O'Connell

Street on the corner of Lower Abbey and Marlborough streets is the **Abbey Theatre** (see page 92; www.abbeytheatre.ie). Founded in 1904 by W.B. Yeats, Lady Augusta Gregory and Edward Martyn, the theatre has long been a showcase for great Irish writing. The early works of Sean O'Casey and John Synge were written for the Abbey. The present theatre dates from 1966, since a fire in 1951 destroyed the original. It now forms part of the National Theatre, along with the Peacock Theatre, its smaller scale stage.

Situated just north of the Abbey Theatre in Marlborough Street is **St Mary's Pro-Cathedral** (www.procathedral.ie) the main Catholic parish church of the city centre, built between 1816 and 1825. Its somewhat forbidding classical Doric exterior seems to dwarf the street; it was originally designed for O'Connell Street. The domed Renaissance interior is very plain, but the Palestrina choir that sings Mass here on Sundays is anything but, and attracts large numbers of visitors.

It is worth making a detour on the pedestrianised areas of **Henry Street** and **Moore Street**, to see their famous markets and hear the cries of the stallholders. Expect some ribald remarks in broad Dublin accents. Moore Street Market is open Monday to Saturday and specialises in fruit, vegetable and flowers. This area is quickly becoming the multi-ethnic hub of Dublin's growing immigrant community. Alongside the fruit stalls are shops and restaurants selling Russian, African and Chinese specialities.

At the northern end of the street is the 1911 **monument to Parnell** by Augustus St-Gaudens. Notice anything

Joyce statue

At the junction of O'Connell Street and North Earl Street is a statue of James Joyce, walking with a cane in his hand. The Dublin populace know it as the 'Prick with the Stick'.

odd? Yes, he is wearing two overcoats. Apparently he always did.

PARNELL SQUARE

Compared to the Georgian squares south of the Liffey, the area around **Parnell Square** looks rather shabby, but once it was just as fashionable and affluent. On the south side of Parnell Square are the **Rotunda Hospital** and the Gate Theatre. In 1751–55, Richard Castle built the Palladian-style Rotunda, Europe's oldest maternity hospital. The chapel on the first floor, with stained-glass

Moore Street Market

windows and rococo plasterwork, has served at different times as an Assembly Room and a cinema; Charles Dickens also gave readings here. What is now the **Gate Theatre** ㉓ (www.gate-theatre.ie) was built in 1784 and is probably the most beautiful stage in Dublin. The theatre company was founded in 1930 by Michael MacLiammóir and Hilton Edwards, and is still going strong today, with an excellent reputation for international and innovative work. James Mason and Orson Welles began their acting careers here. The theatre is now a popular venue for contemporary music concerts.

The **Garden of Remembrance** on the north side of Parnell Square is dedicated to those who lost their lives in the cause of Irish freedom and features a cruciform lake and Oisín Kelly's beautiful sculpture of the *Children of Lir*.

Across the road from the garden, the **Dublin City Gallery, The Hugh Lane** ㉔ (www.hughlane.ie; Tue–Thur 9.45am–6pm, Fri–Sat 10am–5pm, Sun 11am–5pm, closed Mon; free) occupies a home built for Lord Charlemont by Sir William Chambers. This handsome building is worth seeing for itself alone, as well as for the splendid art collection. Sir Hugh Lane, who died in 1915, bequeathed his collection of paintings to the Irish government and the National Gallery in London. The collection includes works by Manet, Degas and other French impressionists as well as their Irish counterparts. The Post-Impressionist paintings of Jack B. Yeats (brother of the famous poet) are particularly noteworthy. The gallery has also acquired the Studio of Francis Bacon and all its contents, which has been reconstructed here as a permanent exhibit.

Next door, the **Dublin Writers Museum** ㉕ (www.writers museum.com; Mon–Sat 9.45 am–4.45pm, Sun 11am– 4.30pm, June–Aug Mon–Fri 10am–6pm) is an intriguing combination of Georgian exterior and Victorian interior. No one interested in Irish writing and theatre should miss this light and elegant museum covering the long Irish literary tradition, displaying first editions, theatre programmes, correspondence, clothing and other memorabilia, as befits a Unesco City of Literature. The collection begins with medieval Irish writing and ends with Brendan Behan, Liam O'Flaherty and Sean O'Faoláin. There are frequent exhibitions and events, and the Writers Centre provides a place for talk and work. Upstairs is a portrait gallery. There is also a children's room, a bookshop, and a good café.

East of Parnell Square, along North Great George's Street, is the **James Joyce Centre** ㉖ (www.jamesjoyce.ie; Tue–Sat 10am–5pm). This interesting museum and cultural centre is housed in a mansion dating from 1784. The centre contains a library, exhibition rooms, and a study centre devoted to the

The Dublin Writers Museum

great novelist. There is a full programme of events, including lectures, tours of the house and a walking tour of Joycean Dublin. Joyce himself must have known the house as the residence of Mr Denis J. Maginni, 'professor of dancing', who appears several times in the novel *Ulysses*.

PHOENIX PARK

On the banks of the Liffey, just 3km (2 miles) from the bustle of O'Connell Street, lies **Phoenix Park** ❷. Comprising some 709 hectares (1,750 acres) of landscaped gardens, woods, pastures and playing fields, it is the biggest urban park in Europe, a graceful and elegant expanse with fine views of the mountains, much loved by Dubliners since it was first opened to the public in 1747. Black plaques mark self-guided heritage walks and nature trails, while bikes can be hired at the gate lodge.

The oldest building in the park is **Ashtown Castle**, a former papal residence that has been renovated to house the splendid **Phoenix Park Visitor Centre** (www.phoenixpark.ie; daily Apr–Sept 10am–6pm, Oct–Mar 9.30am–5.30pm; free), which presents a video and an excellent two-floor exhibition on the history and wildlife of the park (the park itself is open 24 hrs a day, 7 days a week, all year round). The castle itself comprises an early 17th-century tower house, restored with Irish oak from the park, which is held together without a single nail. Outside there is a young garden maze, marking the outline of the original foundations, and a restful café.

The park also boasts the tallest obelisk in Europe in the 67m (220ft) **Wellington Monument**, erected in 1861 after the victory of Waterloo. The Wicklow granite is faced with plaques cast from captured and melted-down cannon. Not quite as large is the **Papal Cross**, commemorating Pope John Paul II's visit in 1979, when more than one million people gathered to celebrate Mass.

JAMES JOYCE'S DUBLIN

The Irish Catholic novelist, poet and short story-writer James Joyce (1882–1941) is best known for his controversial novel *Ulysses* (1922), which describes in minute detail a day in the life of advertising salesman Leopold Bloom as he makes his way through the city. Dublin had also played a part in two of Joyce's previous works, the short story collection *Dubliners* (1914), and the semi-autobiographical novel *A Portrait of the Artist as a Young Man* (1914–15). Joyce's descriptions of Dublin life in *Dubliners* are as evocative as they are gloomy – his city is one of 'dark muddy lanes' and 'dark dripping gardens'. Stephen Dedalus, the dissolute protagonist of *A Portrait of the Artist*, views Dublin in similarly despairing tones. This contrasts with Joyce's buoyant characterisation of Dublin in *Ulysses* as a vibrant, intellectually stimulating city. However the novel's linguistic complexities and general absence of plot will discourage all but the most determined readers.

The **Phoenix Column**, dating from 1747, stands near the natural spring from which the name of the park is derived. This was the result of an English corruption of the Gaelic *fionn uisce*, meaning 'clear water'.

Occupying more than 26 hectares (66 acres), the **Dublin Zoo**  was founded in 1831 (www.dublinzoo. ie; Mon–Sat from 9am, Sun from 10.30am; closing times vary from 3.30pm in Oct to 6pm from Apr–Sept). The landscaped grounds provide a safe home to more than 700 species, including such

The Wellington Monument

endangered animals as snow leopards and golden lion tamarinds. Decimus Burton, who was also responsible for the park lodges, designed the grounds. A highlight is the African Plains, which provides a spacious home for its large species. The Nakuru Safari tour takes visitors through the area.

Also within the sprawling grounds of the park are the official residence of the Irish president **Áras an Uachtaráin**, which dates from 1751 (guided tours from the visitor centre Sat 10.15am–4.30pm, until 3.30pm in winter), and the US ambassador's residence, an 18th-century house that was formerly the official residence of the Viceroy's chief secretary (not open to the public).

Just to the northwest of Phoenix Park is **Farmleigh House** (www.farmleigh.ie; Mar–Dec Thur–Sun 10am–5pm; free).

This grand estate of 78 acres was bought by the government from the Guinness family and has been carefully refurbished. Today the estate is used to accommodate visiting dignitaries, high-level meetings and for public enjoyment. The interior is beautifully presented and the Victorian Courtyard hosts food markets in the spring and summer.

EXCURSIONS

SOUTH OF THE CITY

As if the city itself did not provide enough options, the countryside around Dublin offers a wealth of possible excursions and day trips. The DART railway, running north and south to nearby seaside towns and villages, offers a scenic trip along the coast. Whether you take the DART north or south, you will find good sandy beaches.

Dún Laoghaire is the major port on the east coast. Ferries across the Irish Sea leave from two state-of-the-art piers. West of the harbour is the ramshackle National Maritime Museum.

GETTING OUT

Bus tours will take you to the various destinations (see page 122), and some are accessible by city bus. Dublin Tourism (www.visitdublin.com) at Suffolk Street has all the information, and can arrange tours. Car hire is available at the same site (see page 117). It is worth hiring a car so you can go at your own pace. The suggestions for excursions in this section can all be done in a day or a half-day from the city; most entries indicate how the destination can be reached. Note that some attractions can only by seen by guided tour, and the last admission to these may be 30 to 45 minutes earlier than the official closing time.

Interior of the Joyce Museum

The penultimate stop on the DART is **Bray** ㉙, a faded seaside resort with a beach and amusement arcades. There are splendid views from Bray Head of the harbour and the mountains. You can take the DART on to its terminus at **Greystones**, a pretty coastal town, or you can walk there along the coast from Bray, though parts of the path are in poor condition.

County Wicklow, also to the south of Dublin, rightly deserves its title, 'Garden of Ireland', with some of the most spectacular scenery in the country: rugged mountains, steep, wooded river valleys, and deep lakes as well as charming villages and some notable mansions and gardens.

JAMES JOYCE MUSEUM

At Sandycove in County Dublin the **James Joyce Museum** ㉚ (www.jamesjoycetower.com; daily 10am–4pm; Nov–Feb by appointment only) is one of the most unusual small museums in or around Dublin. It is housed in a Martello Tower; a series of such towers, some 12m (40ft) high and 2.5m (8ft) thick,

> ### St Kevin
>
> St Kevin, founder of the monastery at Glendalough, was famed for his patience. One story tells how a bird laid an egg in the palm of his hand. To avoid causing harm, the holy man stayed still until the egg hatched.

were constructed along the coast at the beginning of the 19th century to guard against invasion by Napoleon. Joyce actually lived in the tower only very briefly, and it is the location for the first chapter of Ulysses. Full of Joycean memorabilia (including his guitar and waistcoat), correspondence, and rare editions of books and manuscripts, it is a shrine for Joyce enthusiasts. DART to Glasthule.

AVOCA

The picturesque village of **Avoca** ③ in County Wicklow became famous as the setting for the BBC TV series *Ballykissangel*. A company of handweavers has been working here since at least 1723, and visitors are able to watch them as they work. Unfortunately, though, their products are somewhat less distinctive since the place became a popular tourist attraction. There is a colourful shop and a popular café in the small complex of traditional buildings (daily, summer 9am–6pm, winter 9.30am–5.30pm).

GLENDALOUGH

Set in a beautiful landscape, with clear lakes and streams surrounded by steep wooded hills, the sacred site of **Glendalough** ③ (from the Irish for 'Valley of the Two Lakes', or Gleann Dá Locha) in the Wicklow Mountains, is still highly evocative, and should not be missed. It was the place chosen by St Kevin for a monastery that over the centuries, became a great spiritual centre of learning, attracting pilgrims from all over Europe. Despite Viking raids, a great fire at the end of the

14th century and long years of neglect, many of the original buildings still stand at Glendalough: the 11th-century round tower (30m/100ft high and 15m/50ft around the base), a 9th-century barrel-vaulted church known as 'St Kevin's Kitchen', and the roofless cathedral. There are also scores of Celtic crosses here.

The site can be visited by car or bus tour, or by taking St Kevin's bus from the north side of St Stephen's Green, opposite the Mansion House in Dawson Street (www.glendalough bus.com; leave 11.30am, arrive 12.50pm, return 4.30pm). The visitor centre (mid-Mar–mid-Oct, daily 9.30am–7pm, mid-Oct–mid-Mar until 5pm; www.heritageireland.com) provides a 20-minute audiovisual presentation of the history

Glendalough is a big draw for tourists

of Irish monasticism, plus an exhibition on the geology and wildlife of the area, and conducts guided tours, but you can also wander about on your own. Glendalough's three nature trails take under an hour's relaxed walking. Glendalough is part of the **Wicklow Mountains National Park** ㊳, an area of about 200 sq km (78 sq miles), which includes most of upland Wicklow, with spectacular scenery, wildlife and rare flora. The 137km (85-mile) **Wicklow Way** long-distance footpath wends its course through the park.

MOUNT USHER GARDENS

In 1868 the Walpole family established the spectacular **Mount Usher Gardens** ❸❹ (www.mountushergardens.ie; Mar–Oct daily 10. am– 5pm; car or bus tours). The climate and soil are such that plants and trees that would not normally survive this far north are capable of flourishing, explaining the enormous variety of more than 4,000 plants, trees and shrubs from all over the world. The 8-hectare (20-acre) paradise is near Ashford, along the River Vartry. It attracts a range of birds and wildfowl. There is a shopping courtyard and Avoca Garden Café on site.

POWERSCOURT

About 18km (12 miles) from Dublin, outside the pretty village of Enniskerry in the foothills of the Wicklow Mountains, is **Powerscourt House and Gardens** ❸❺ (www.powerscourt. ie; daily 9.30am–5.30pm, gardens close at dusk in winter; guided tours available). The gardens are among the greatest in Europe, and take in a view of the Sugar Loaf Mountain as part of their design. Powerscourt consists of some 5,500 hectares (14,000 acres), hugging the River Dargle. The enormous Palladian house was destroyed by fire in 1974. It now incorporates the restored ballroom, a restaurant overlooking the gardens, an exhibition on the history of the estate, several shops and a garden centre.

The formal splendour of the grounds testifies to the 18th-century desire to tame nature, but it is done with such superlative results that one can only be thankful that the work was undertaken. The sweeping terraces offer magnificent views; statuary rears up out of ornamental lakes; deer roam the parklands; and the Dargle obligingly throws itself over 122m (400ft) of rock to form the highest waterfall in Ireland (4km/2.5 miles from the main estate). Children like the pets' cemetery.

RUSSBOROUGH HOUSE 36

This magnificent Georgian-Palladian house at Blessington is one of the earliest Irish great houses (www.russboroughhouse.ie; guided tours only, May–Sept daily 10am–5pm, Apr and Oct Sun and holidays 10am–5pm). The building was designed by Richard Castle and constructed on a monumental scale in 1740–1750. 213m (700ft) facade of Wicklow granite, Doric arcades and wonderful ornamentation are all set against an impressive terraced landscape, with the extensive grounds covering some 80 hectares (200 acres).

The grandiose Powerscourt Estate

Irish country houses are generally distinguished by their architecture rather than their contents, but Russborough is a striking exception to this rule. The interiors feature superb plasterwork by the Francini brothers, identifiable, as elsewhere, by their trademark of eagles' heads. The plasterwork on the staircase is extraordinary, with its lavish swags of flowers gently held in the mouths of some very patient-looking dogs. The inlaid floors are particularly lovely, and there are extensive collections of furniture, silver and tapestries.

Also in the house is the impressive **Beit Collection** of paintings, which is shared with the National Gallery; it includes celebrated works by Gainsborough, Goya, Guardi, Hals, Reynolds,

The trawler dock at Howth

Rubens, Velasquez, Vermeer and others, plus a series of eight paintings by Murillo depicting the story of the prodigal son.

WEST OF THE CITY

When William Connolly, then speaker of the Irish House of Commons, set his heart on a palatial country home, he turned to Italian architect Alessandro Galilei. In 1722, he designed the facade of **Castletown House ③⑦**, at Celbridge, County Kildare (www.castletownhouse.ie; Mid-Mar–end Oct Tue–Sun 10am–6pm, also bank holidays, additional Christmas opening, last tour at 4.45pm, parklands: daily during daylight hours; car or bus 67/67A followed by a half-mile walk). The Irishman Edward Lovett Pearce, who finished this Palladian master-piece, is responsible for the colonnades and side pavilions. The result is one of the most graceful and distinctive houses of the period in Ireland. The house's famous Long Gallery has Pompeii fresco-inspired designs and Venetian chande-liers; the great staircase is the work of Simon Vierpyl; and the plasterwork is by the Francinis. A 48m (140ft) high obelisk adorns the grounds, which are now sadly encroached upon.

IRISH NATIONAL STUD AND JAPANESE GARDENS

Horses are immensely popular in Ireland, and County Kildare can claim to be at the heart of horse country. The Curragh and Punchestown racecourses are situated here, and the **Irish National Stud** ❸❽ at Tully (www.irishnationalstud.ie; mid-Feb–Dec daily 9.30am–5pm; combined ticket covers Irish Stud, Irish Horse Museum, Japanese Gardens and St Fiachras Garden). Home to breeding stallions, the national stud has produced some of the most successful horses in the country. Visitors see horses being trained and exercised. There is also a museum illustrating the history of the horse in Ireland, which features the skeleton of the racehorse Arkle.

Adjacent to the stud are the **Japanese Gardens**, created by the stud's founder in the early part of the century, and well worth a visit, and the **St Fiachras Garden**, created to celebrate the millennium.

NORTH OF THE CITY

To the north of Dublin, the DART will take you to the **Howth** ❸❾ peninsula, which affords splendid views along a cliff-top coastal walk above the pretty fishing village. In early summer nesting sea birds abound, as well as interesting land birds and butterflies attracted by the moorland terrain of the cliff top. In July and August there is a wonderful colour combination of purple heather and yellow gorse. When walking up to the lighthouse, it is difficult to believe that Dublin is just a few miles away–until you see Dublin Bay spread out before you. Also located in Howth is the **National Transport Museum** (www.nationaltransportmuseum.org; Jun–Aug Mon–Sat 10am–5pm, Sept–May Sat–Sun 2–5pm) at Howth Castle.

Malahide Castle

NATIONAL BOTANIC GARDENS

Originally modelled on London's Kew Gardens, Ireland's premier horticultural attraction is the **National Botanic Gardens** ④ at Glasnevin (Nov–Feb daily 9am–4.30pm, Mar–Oct, daily 9am–6pm; glasshouse until 5pm Mon–Fri, 5.45pm Sat–Sun; free; www.botanicgardens.ie). A short bus ride (nos. 4 or 9) north of O'Connell Street, it was established by the Royal Dublin Society in 1795. With over 20,000 species in more than 20 hectares (50 acres) of grounds, there is plenty to see and enjoy in any season. Built between 1843 and 1868, the four magnificently restored glasshouse groups include an alpine house, a palm and orchid house, and the Curvilinear Range, a spectacular curving glass-house of cast iron.

Nearby is the **Glasnevin Cemetery Museum** (www.glasnevinmuseum.ie; Mon–Fri 10am–5pm, Sat–Sun 11am–5pm; tours daily 11am and 2pm), a striking new visitor centre, introducing Dublin's main cemetery, where some of the most notable figures in recent Irish history are buried. These include Charles Stewart Parnell, Daniel O'Connell and Éamon de Valera.

CASINO MARINO

Located on the Malahide Road 3 miles (5km) from the centre of Dublin, Lord Charlemont's 'small house by the sea' is regarded as the finest neoclassical building in Ireland. Built in 1762–77, it was the masterpiece of William Chambers and is a work of great ingenuity. From the outside it looks like a small Greek-style temple, but is in fact two storeys high and contains eight rooms. To preserve the harmonious design the four corner columns are hollow to carry water off the roof, and the urns on the roof are disguised chimneys. The interior has exquisite floors and plasterwork (mid-Mar–Oct daily 10am–5pm).

The **Casino Marino** ⓐ still stands in perfect splendour on a gentle rise. Down the road is 'Spite Crescent', built by an enemy of Lord Charlemont to spoil his view from the Casino. It was here that Bram Stoker stayed while writing *Dracula* in 1897.

MALAHIDE CASTLE
The crenellated **Malahide Castle and Gardens** ⓐ (www.malahidecastleandgardens.ie; daily, 9.30am–5.30pm) is set in the pretty seaside town of Malahide (DART station). Home to the Talbot family for 800 years, parts of the building date back to the 12th century. The castle, now publicly owned, contains fine 18th-century furniture and displays on the family's history. The 22 acres of ornamental gardens, planted by the Talbot family, contain over 5000 species, fully labelled. There is also a playground, pitch and putt and an Avoca café.

Brendan Behan's grave at Glasnevin Cemetery

NEWBRIDGE HOUSE AND TRADITIONAL FARM
Newbridge House ⓐ (Apr–Sept daily 9am–5pm; Oct–Mar Tue–Sun 10am–4pm) and its

The huge prehistoric mound at Newgrange

estate of some 142 hectares (350 acres) at Donabate, County Dublin, belonged to the Cobbe family from 1736. The beautifully restored house contains some interesting furniture and plasterwork, and there is also a courtyard incorporating several artisans' cottages with period furniture and tools, a forge and stables, and a working farm with cows, draught horses, ponies, donkeys, goats, hens and ducks.

NEWGRANGE

Newgrange ㊹ is the most important of the prehistoric sites around Dublin, located about 3km (2 miles) east of Slane in County Meath. Access is solely by tour from the **Brú na Bóinne Visitor Centre** (www.heritageireland.ie; Nov–Jan, 9.30am–5pm, Feb–Apr & Oct, 9.30am–5.30pm, May & mid-Sept–end-Sept 9am–6.30pm, June–mid-Sept 9am–7pm). Newgrange is the best-preserved passage tomb in Europe, 500 years older than the Pyramids (3000BC) and 1,000 years more ancient than Stonehenge. Built around 3200, Newgrange may be the world's oldest solar observatory – the whole edifice is aligned in such a way that for several days of the winter solstice, light from the sun floods the inner chamber for around 17 minutes, causing a spectacular effect. The guide on the tour attempts to give an idea of this effect by plunging the chamber into darkness and slowly bringing up the light. The sites are busy in summer, and entry cannot be guaranteed. Go early in the day, and allow at least three hours.

Nearby is **Knowth** ⓮, an even larger and older complex, which dates back to the early Neolithic and has two passage graves.

TARA

Tara ⓰, situated south of the busy town of Navan in County Meath, is a familiar name in Celtic myths and legends. The site was the cultural, political and religious centre of early Celtic civilisation and is reputedly where the high kings had their palace. However, its importance waned after the arrival of Christianity, and nowadays there is little to see except the hill, the remains of an Iron-Age fort, some pillar stones and the rewarding views over the central Irish plain. In a nearby 19th-century Anglican church is the **visitor centre** (late May–Oct daily 9.30am–6pm), with exhibits and an audio-visual show. Guided tours are available – they begin at the visitors' centre and lead past earthworks and ditches with evocative names such as *Rath na Riogh* (Fort of the Kings) and *Dumha Na nGiall* (Ditch of the Hostages).

Winter lottery

The overwhelming demand to see Newgrange during the winter solstice has forced Irish Heritage to hold a lottery. Visitors can sign up in the welcome centre. Or you can email your postal address and contact phone number to brunaboinne@opw.ie and they'll enter your name. From an average 35,000 entries, 50 names are chosen.

WHAT TO DO

Dublin is rapidly becoming a 24-hour city, so there is plenty to enjoy when your sightseeing is done. The city's many pubs are the centre of social life, offering conversation and a quiet pint, food, music and song. There are also lots of late-night clubs and bars. With first-class shops and a profusion of booksellers, galleries and antiques dealers, you can browse or buy contentedly. If you are feeling active, there are also some excellent opportunities for sports.

PUBS

As you walk through Dublin's streets it will sometimes seem that there is a pub on every corner. Pubs are Ireland's living rooms – they provide not only drink and food, but atmosphere, entertainment and amusing talk. You may not fall into conversation in Dublin quite as readily as in a country pub, but you will find that here, as everywhere, the Irish are welcoming hosts. Most pubs also serve food – they are good places to have lunch – and some have dining rooms. Pubs in the O'Connell Street and Temple Bar area now have security guards on the door, vetting customers to ensure a pleasant experience for all. Pubs open at 11am and close at 12.30am, though many pubs in central Dublin stay open later at weekends.

The oldest pub in Dublin is reputedly the Brazen Head (Bridge Street Lower) where, it is claimed, a tavern has stood since the 12th century. Wolfe Tone and his United

> ### Time to settle
>
> When you order a Guinness, the bartender fills the glass three quarters and lets it settle before topping it off. Do the same before you take a drink. It should be a smooth, dark black before you tip it back.

The local tipple

Irishmen are believed to have met here to plan their rebellion. It is cosy and intimate, with a cobblestone courtyard, and a good pint of Guinness served at the bar. Other authentic old Dublin pubs include Toner's (Lower Baggot Street), Mulligan's (Poolbeg Street), Ryan's (Parkgate Street) and the Long Hall (South Great George's Street), reputedly the city's longest bar.

Whatever you are looking for in a pub, Dublin will gladly provide. If you are after traditional music, O'Donoghue's (Merrion Row) and The Temple Bar (see below) are still among Dublin's best; O'Donoghue's was formerly the haunt of The Dubliners. The traditional Slattery's (Capel Street) has been restyled to give it a chic and modern look, appealing to trendy clubbers, while the renovated Jack Nealon's (also in Capel Street) has jazz on Sunday and eclectic music the rest of the week. If you like traditional dancing, go to O'Shea's Merchant (Bridge

Irish pubs are the best place to meet and greet locals

Street Lower). The Stag's Head (Dame Court) is known for its good food and wonderful old wooden interior.

Off Grafton Street is Kehoe's (South Anne Street), a favourite watering hole. On Duke Street are two pubs with Ulysses connections – Davy Byrne's, where Leopold Bloom ate a gorgonzola sandwich and drank a glass of wine, and Bailey's, a busy, trendy and gay-friendly bar on the site of Leopold Bloom's house. Behind the Gaiety Theatre, you will probably encounter a theatrical crowd in Neary's (Chatham Street). Microbreweries have also appeared in Ireland, and the Dublin produce can be sampled at the Porterhouse Brewing Company (Parliament Street).

There are many old pubs in Temple Bar, but they are often twee and tourist choked. If you fancy a pint, then opt for some of the least offensive including the Oliver St John Gogarty (Fleet Street), named for the man-of-letters who was the model for a character in Ulysees, which has good traditional and other music. There's music upstairs in the small, quaint Ha'penny Bridge Inn (Wellington Quay). The Temple Bar (Temple Bar) attracts a busy, lively crowd; The Norseman (East Essex Street) is favoured by the art crowd, while the Auld Dubliner (Anglesea Street) is a pleasant pub that caters a lot for tourists. Make sure to drop in to the elegant old Palace on Fleet Street; with its beautiful interior and buzzy atmosphere it's popular with journalists from the nearby *Irish Times*. Doheny & Nesbitt's on Baggot Street is famous for political debate, while cabinet ministers, legal eagles and journalists in search of visiting celebrities favour the Horseshoe Bar at the Shelbourne Hotel.

If you are after a taste of modern Dublin, then there are chic, sleek pubs dotted throughout the city. The Market Bar (Fade Street) is an enormous bar and tapas restaurant that oozes charm despite its size.

SHOPPING

The main shopping areas are in and around Grafton Street, and north of the river in O'Connell Street and Henry Street. Pedestrian Grafton Street is lined with well-known chains, plus the excellent, upmarket Brown Thomas department store. Smaller, hipper boutiques have sprung up in the former rag trade district west of Grafton Street, known as the Creative Quarter. O'Connell Street has more downmarket shops, but two landmarks are still here: Eason's for books and art supplies, and Arnotts department store on adjoining Henry Street.

Shoppers on Grafton Street

SHOPPING CENTRES

St Stephen's Green Shopping Centre is at the bottom of Grafton Street overlooking the famous urban park. It has three floors of shops, but none really stand out and many are chains. It is worth a look if you need to pick up something in the large and good value Dunnes Stores, with homewares, men's, women's and kids fashion and a supermarket. There is also a large Boots chemist and a branch of Hughes and Hughes bookstores. The **Powerscourt Townhouse** on Clarendon Street (follow the sign from Grafton Street) is at the core of the Creative

Quarter, and is a historic building with four floors of restaurants and cafés, and antiques, jewellery and designer clothing. Also on Clarendon Street is the smaller, upmarket **Westbury Mall**, with cafés, clothing shops, accessories and jewellery shops. Further along, you will find Drury Street and South William Street with some good quirky shops including classic rainwear at Francis Campelli, and Dublin's best vintage store Jenny Vander (Drury Street). At Castle Market make sure to pop in for a browse around the elegant designer boutique Costume and the sophisticated Helen McAlinden store, with its classic, minimalist approach to women's designs.

On the other side of Grafton Street, leading into Dawson Street, the **Royal Hibernian Way** is another small shopping mall with some exclusive shops. Dawson Street is lined with bookshops and boutiques. North of the river, the **Jervis Centre** on Henry Street has a selection of shops and department stores, including many UK chains. At the **ILAC Centre**, also on Henry Street, you will find numerous clothes shops and a large branch of Dunnes Stores, an Irish clothing and groceries chain.

MARKETS

Dublin's oldest market is on **Moore Street** (Mon–Sat). The market is famous for the cries of its sellers, on whom the well-known song Molly Malone is modelled. Fruit, vegetables, electronics and a little bit of everything else are on sale here. It is also the place to go to pick up ethnic food and goods.

Pretty **George's Street Arcade** (Mon–Sat) is a covered market between South Great George's and Drury streets. Shops and stalls line this atmospheric little market – a good place for second-hand books, art, music, vintage clothing and a variety of ethnic ware.

The **Temple Bar Food Market** (Sat 10am–4.30pm) at Meeting House Square is great for speciality foods and gourmet

Temple Bar Food Market

delights. It's also worth heading to the Old City section of Temple Bar where you will find a good range of chic interiors stores, plus the Gutter Bookshop – one of Dublin's finest – and the trendy Cow's Lane Fashion and Design Mart (mid-Mar–Oct Sat only 10am–5pm) with its innovative designers. The Saturday fashion and food market in and around Cow's Lane is one of the city's best. In addition, on Saturday and Sunday, **Blackrock Market** (Sat and Sun 11am-5pm; on Main Street, near Blackrock DART station) has stalls selling jewellery, designer crafts, books, antiques and clothes.

WHAT TO BUY

Antiques. Don't miss a stroll down Francis Street, Dublin's 'antiques highway' and lined with antiques and art stores. These include Michael Connell Antiques, specialising in Victorian and Edwardian furniture, silver, brassware and china; Martin Fennelley's shop selling decorative art, fine furniture, paintings and lamps; and Johnston Antiques' fine Irish and Georgian antiques. Also check out the lovely antiques shops on the second floor of Powerscourt Townhouse and stalls in Georges Street Arcade.

Art. For contemporary art, you should try the Kerlin Gallery (off South Anne Street), the Taylor Galleries (Kildare Street), or the Oliver Sears Gallery (Molesworth Street). The Temple Bar Gallery (Temple Bar) exhibits the work of contemporary artists and the Oriel Gallery on Clare Street has an equally impressive and more accessible collection of original art for sale.

Books. Eason's on O'Connell Street is a huge shop with mainstream books, magazines, newspapers and art supplies. Hodges Figgis (of Ulysses fame) on Dawson Street carries an excellent selection of literature, general books, books on Ireland, and the works of Irish writers. International Books in South Frederick Street specialises in languages. For antiquarian books, go to Ulysses Rare Books in Duke Street. In Temple Bar, the Gallery of Photography has a bookshop, while Books Upstairs on College Green has an interesting selection of Irish titles including poetry. The labyrinthine Winding Stair on Ormond Quay is an interesting second-hand bookshop beneath a restaurant.

Chocolates. Delicious Irish handmade chocolates can be bought at Butler's Chocolate Café in Grafton Street.

Crafts. The most distinguished place for modern Irish crafts is DESIGNyard in Frederick Street with its outstanding selection of jewellery, sculpture and contemporary design. The Irish Celtic Craftshop (Lord Edward Street) offers more traditional crafts. The Kilkenny Shop (Nassau Street) is a good hunting ground for everything from John Rocha-designed Waterford Crystal to Orla Kiely designer wellies and Aran jumpers.

Ireland has long been known for its fine crystal, with famous brands including Waterford Crystal, Cavan, Galway, Tipperary and Tyrone Crystal. Irish designers John Rocha and Louise Kennedy have designed more contemporary lines for Waterford and Tipperary Crystal respectively. Prices do not vary. Try the House of Ireland (Nassau Street). The larger department stores, such as Brown Thomas on Grafton Street, are good places to find designer crystal lines.

Family Crests. There are a vast number of shops specialising in coats of arms on everything from plaques to keychains. Try Heraldic Artists and House of Names, both on Nassau Street.

Food. The Irish supermarket chain, Dunnes Stores (outlets on Middle Abbey Street, St Stephen's Green Shopping Centre, the ILAC Centre) sells Irish smoked salmon: ask for the wild, not farmed, variety. For Irish country cheeses, go to Sheridan Cheesemongers on South Anne Street or Listons in Harcourt, Lower Hamden Street

Knitwear. There are two kinds of knits for sale: expensive traditional handknit sweaters and sweaters 'handknit' (that is to say, hand-loomed) on a machine. For the former, go to the House of Ireland on Nassau Street. For the latter, bargains can be found at Blarney Woollen Mills (Nassau Street). The Kilkenny Shop on Nassau Street carries a large variety of knitwear and handwoven goods. Monaghan's (Royal Hibernian Way) specialises in cashmere for men. Bringing knitting right into the 21st century is This is Knit (Powerscourt Townhouse), which has a fabulous range of wool and patterns.

Linens. Brown Thomas has a great linen department, as does Murphy Sheehy (Castle Market).

Music. For Irish music, Spindizzy Records (32 Market Arcade, South Great George's Street) and Claddagh Records (Cecilia Street, Temple Bar) carry a good selection of traditional Irish and other Irish recordings. You can't miss Tower Records on Wicklow Street.

Photography. If you're looking for memory cards, batteries and photo printers, any of the following should be of

Kitsch souvenirs of a stay in Dublin

help: Hall Cameras on Talbot Street, One Hour Photo on St Stephens Green North, or the Camera Centre on Grafton Street. For used as well as new equipment, try the Dublin Camera Exchange on South Great Georges Street.

Pottery and Porcelain. In Nassau Street the Kilkenny Shop has a fine selection.

Souvenirs. Shopping for souvenirs should be an easy task in Dublin. Nassau Street is the best destination for souvenir shopping on the fly. Some shops may not be too original, but they have all the trinkets folks back home will be happy to get their hands on. If you have more time, there are some excellent shops spread throughout the city showcasing Irish crafts and design.

Toys. In Dublin, Avoca (www.avoca.com) and Arnotts (www.arnotts.ie) both have extensive toy departments.

Wine. For a tasty alternative to the world of Guinness and whiskey, try Mitchell and Sons in the CHQ Building and Glasthule Rd, or Berry Bros & Rudd on St. James's Street.

ENTERTAINMENT

THEATRE

Dublin has a proud tradition in theatre, which is still very much alive, so advance booking is advisable. The **Abbey Theatre** in Lower Abbey Street is Ireland's national theatre (see also below). Once on the cutting edge, today its more experimental repertoire is presented on its second, basement

IRELAND'S NATIONAL THEATRE

Dublin's first theatre opened in 1637, and thereafter the city produced many notable playwrights, including Sheridan, Goldsmith, Wilde and Shaw. However, there was nothing particularly 'Irish' about their work. W. B. Yeats wanted to create a distinctly Irish theatre of poetic drama, and he turned for inspiration to the legends of ancient Ireland. He looked for a backer, and found Lady Augusta Gregory, who became his partner. Their first productions were done on a shoestring, wherever they could find a space. Finally, in 1904, they acquired a theatre of their own, and the Abbey was born.

The Abbey's career was not without controversy. J. M. Synge's play, The *Playboy of the Western World*, now recognised as a masterpiece, provoked a riot when it was first staged. Later on, *The Plough and the Stars*, by the Abbey's first great realist playwright, Sean O'Casey, caused similar public outrage, and the police were called to protect the theatre.

After Yeats's death in 1939, the Abbey entered a period of limbo, although its acting tradition continued to be world renowned. Things turned around with the opening of its new theatre in 1966 and the emergence of new Irish playwrights – Brian Friel, Conor McPherson, and Frank McGuinness among others. Today, the Abbey continues its tradition of commitment to new work by Irish authors in both English and Gaelic.

stage, the intimate **Peacock**. The **Gate Theatre** in Parnell Square, has a similar tradition, and stages a cosmopolitan mix of Irish and international theatre plus musical acts. It is known for showcasing important new Irish playwrights.

The Gate Theatre

The Victorian **Olympia** in Dame Street is the venue for all sorts of popular theatre, concerts and variety shows. The **Gaiety Theatre** in South King Street is worth visiting for its ornate décor alone. It runs a range of productions from plays to variety acts. For innovative theatre, the **Project Arts Centre** in East Essex Street has a lively programme of dance, drama, and performance arts, while **Andrew's Lane** also puts on modern productions. The **Samuel Beckett Theatre** at Trinity College is mainly for drama students. Theatre productions, opera and ballet, and major international acts feature at the splendid Daniel Libeskind-designed theatre in Grand Canal Square, part of the Docklands development, currently known by it's sponsor's name as the Bord Gáis Energy Theatre.

Other theatres of note include the **Civic Theatre** outside the city in Tallaght, with its broad repertoire of music, drama and comedy productions and the **O2** entertainment venue. The **Lambert Puppet Theatre** in Monkstown is popular with children. The most important event of the theatre season is the **Dublin Theatre Festival**, held in September–October each year. A fringe festival precedes this event annually.

COMEDY

The International Bar on Wicklow Street has started the careers of many Irish comedians and is still going strong. The revamped Laughter Lounge at Eden Quay is Ireland's premier comedy spot with gigs on Thursday, Friday and Saturday nights.

CLASSICAL MUSIC AND OPERA

The National Symphony Orchestra can be heard in a year-round programme of concerts at the **National Concert Hall** (NCH) in Earlsfort Terrace. The NCH also hosts jazz and traditional music evenings. Chamber music concerts and recitals are given at the **Irish Museum of Modern Art** at the beautiful Royal Hospital building in Kilmainham. **St Anne's Church** on Dawson Street has lunchtime concerts. Dublin Castle, St Patrick's Cathedral and

TRADITIONAL MUSIC

The word *seisiún* – meaning an impromptu evening of music and song, usually in a pub – has a particular resonance for the Irish, and there is plenty of opportunity in Dublin to enjoy traditional Irish sounds. A *seisiún* may start when someone – probably the innocent-looking man sitting in the corner huddled over a pint of Guinness – produces a guitar as if from nowhere, and his neighbour responds by bringing out a well-concealed *bodhrán* (goatskin traditional Irish drum). Soon everyone is joining in.

The mainstay of traditional music is the fiddle. The guitar is something of a latecomer, having arrived around the 1960s, but it is now well established. Other instruments you may hear are the *uillean* pipes (softer than the Scottish bagpipe), the six-hole wooden flute, the tin whistle, the accordion and the banjo, a 19th-century transfer from America.

While the real centre of traditional music is in the west, you will find it played in pubs across Dublin; watch for listings or signs in the pubs.

the High Lane Gallery host occasional concerts. Another venue for classical music is the huge **Helix** complex at the Dublin City University campus on Collins Avenue. Dublin also has a number of music festivals (see page 99).

Irish flautist

Opera Ireland offers short spring and winter seasons based on the standard repertoire at the **Gaiety Theatre** in King Street. The small but enterprising Opera Theatre Company does two or three performances a year of short operas by contemporary Irish or baroque composers.

ROCK, FOLK AND JAZZ

One of Dublin's largest venues is the O2, East Link Bridge, which hosts major pop and rock acts (the smash hit *Riverdance* was staged here). The RDS in Ballsbridge also occasionally holds huge open-air concerts. *The Irish Times* carries listings for all such events in its Friday supplement, *The Ticket*, and the *Evening Herald* has up-to-the-minute information (or see www.entertainment.ie). Some of the best music is heard at the mid-size venues: the **Olympia Theatre**, the **Ambassador** (O'Connell Street), Vicar Street (off Thomas Street), and **the Button Factory** in Curved Street, Temple Bar, where you can hear everything from local acts to international artists. **Whelans** on Wexford Street is a good place to hear up-and-coming artists while the Sugar Club on Leeson Street is a plush and stylish spot for all sorts of live music from jazz and blues to Latin. Jazz fans should check out one of the city's oldest jazz venues JJ Smyth's (Aungier Street) with nightly gigs.

A night on the town

DANCE

Dublin has a number of modern dance and ballet companies that perform at various venues. For traditional Irish dancing, go to **O'Shea's Merchant** (Bridge Street Lower). **Cultúrlann na hÉireann** holds concerts, stage shows and traditional dances in Monkstown (www.comhaltas.ie).

FILM

The historical **Savoy Cinema** in O'Connell Street is the main city centre location for the big new-release cinemas. Art-house and international films are shown at the **Irish Film Institute**, in Eustace Street, whose two cinemas present a varied programme of new international and archival films. In summer, open-air movies are screened in Meeting House Square in Temple Bar.

NIGHTCLUBS

Nightclubs tend to come and go, so it is essential to check the listings in local publications like *The Ticket*, or online at http://Dublin.lecool.com.

Leeson Street was always a popular spot for late-night dance clubs, but now the 'strip' is dotted with lap-dancing clubs, attracting an older clientele. However, some of the old haunts like Leggs remain, and the Sugar Club is a lively music venue. Dublin's beautiful people flock to **Lillies Bordello**

(Adam Court, Grafton Street), but it does have a relatively strict door policy. RiRa, a basement venue under the Globe pub on Dame Street, attracts a younger, trendy crowd.

SPORTS

GOLF

Golf is extremely popular, and there are many superb courses in and around Dublin. The Royal Golf Club at Dollymount and many other clubs welcome visitors. For further information, contact Dublin Tourism, the **Golfing Union of Ireland** (www.gui.ie), or go to www.discoverireland.com/golf.

FISHING

Sea angling is permitted all year, but river fishing requires a licence. Information can be obtained from Dublin Tourism or any fishing shop.

SPECTATOR SPORTS

The traditional Irish games of **hurling** and **Gaelic football** are played at Croke Park. **Horse racing** takes place at Leopardstown; at the Curragh (flat racing) and Punchestown (National Hunt racing) in County Kildare. The premiere **show jumping** event is the Dublin Horse Show at the RDS. **Greyhound racing** is on at Shelbourne Park, Ringsend, and at Harold's Cross Stadium. **Rugby** and international **football** (soccer) are played at Lansdowne Road in Ballsbridge.

WATERSPORTS/BEACHES

Although there are beaches at Malahide and Dollymount, the very best ones are in the south, at Bray and Killiney. At Sandycove there's the **Forty Foot** bathing spot, which was once a men's nude beach, but is now open to everyone. It is not advisable to swim within 8km (5 miles) of the city centre because of pollution.

DUBLIN FOR CHILDREN

There are plenty of things for children to enjoy in Dublin. Note that family tickets are available for rail and bus services and that children under 16 travel at half-fare on buses and DART.

The Ark, on Eustace Street in Temple Bar, is a cultural centre that offers a changing programme of plays, workshops, readings and performances, all geared towards youngsters. It is best to book in advance (tel: 01 670 7788; www.ark.ie). The **Lambert Puppet Theatre** in Monkstown stages panto-style plays geared for young audiences (www.lambertpuppet theatre.ie). **Imaginosity** in Sandyford (tel: 01 217 6130; www. imaginosity.ie) is a fun and educational space for children.

Museums that will appeal to children include the **Natural History Museum** (see page 55) and the **National Wax Museum in** Foster Place. There are nature trails in **Phoenix Park** and the **Dublin Zoo** has a pet corner and zoo train (see page 69).

Older children should enjoy **Dublinia** (see page 46), a lively recreation of medieval 'Diflin'. The self-guided **Rock 'n' Stroll Trail** around Dublin, which follows in the footsteps of Irish rock legends, should appeal particularly to the teenage crowd. Also popular are the **Viking Splash Tours** (start point St Stephen's Green; www. vikingsplash.ie), an adventurous tour by land and water in an amphibious vehicle.

Children will enjoy a Viking Splash Tour

FESTIVALS AND EVENTS

February/March Rugby Six Nations Championships: Landsdowne Road, Ballsbridge. Dublin International Film Festival.

March St Patrick's Day Parade.

April Handel's Messiah commemorative concert, held in Temple Bar on the 13th April – the anniversary of its premiere in 1742.

April/May Gumball Rally - Gumball 3000 organises a luxury automotive rally in which 100 of the world's most spectacular supercars will drive 3000 miles in seven days.

May International Dance Festival Ireland: various venues, a range of contemporary dance performances from top companies around the world. The Camden Crawls host over 150 music and live comedy acts in city centre venues to showcase up and coming talent. Dublin Gay Theatre Festival.

June Bloomsday: Dublin city centre. A celebration of Joyce and Ulysses, held in city streets and parks, and at the Joyce Museum, Sandycove. Bloom: a flower-show and gardening extravaganza held in the Phoenix Park. Taste of Dublin: A four-day celebration of food and drink in the Iveagh Gardens. Waterways Ireland Docklands Maritime Summer Festival brings sailing, kayaking, windsurfing and a canal barge gathering to the urban setting of Docklands' Grand Canal Square. Dublin Kite Festival.

July Oxegen Festival: various venues. This two-day rock festival is one of the biggest events on the Irish music calendar. Street Performance World Championships: street performers from all over the world compete in Merrion Square. The Dun Laoghaire Festival of World Cultures: a fantastic celebration of global culture, music and dance.

August Dublin Horse Show: RDS, Ballsbridge.

September All-Ireland Hurling and Football Finals: Croke Park. Dublin Fringe Festival: offbeat sister to the main theatre festival.

September/October Dublin Theatre Festival.

October Dublin City Marathon: a run through the historic streets.

December National Crafts Fair of Ireland: RDS, Ballsbridge. Leopardstown Christmas Racing Festival: a four-day festival end December.

EATING OUT

The days of overcooked cabbage, mountains of boiled potatoes, and cholesterol-laden fried meat are long gone in Dublin. Not only is there a new Irish cuisine, created by imaginative young chefs, but ethnic restaurants of all kinds give a wider choice than ever before.

Of course, Dublin has always had the fresh ingredients for a fine cuisine. Situated as it is on the broad sweep of Dublin Bay, with the waters of the Atlantic nearby and a plethora of streams and rivers, the city has access to both sea and freshwater fish in abundance. Here you will find succulent oysters, freshly caught lobster and crab, wild salmon, sole and pike. Tender lamb comes from Kerry and Wicklow; country cheeses, made on farms and in monasteries have begun to achieve a worldwide reputation. Irish breads, apple tarts and fruitcakes have always been delicious, as has traditional Irish cuisine, though it is prepared now with greater delicacy and lightness of touch.

MEALS AND MEAL TIMES

Breakfast is either the 'continental' variety – fruit juice, bread, cereals, coffee or tea – or traditional Irish, which generally means robust portions of fried eggs, bacon, tomatoes and sausages, black and white pudding and bread, washed down with coffee or strong tea. Most hotels and restaurants serve breakfast from around 7 or 8am until about 10am.

Lunch is from around noon until 2.30 or 3pm. Many of the more expensive restaurants offer three or four course set lunches, but you can also find simple salads, sandwiches or hot meals at most pubs, cafés and snack-bars. Most cafés serve snacks and light meals all day from 8.30 or 9am until 6pm, though many stay open as late as 1 or 2am.

The elegant Café en Seine, on Dawson Street

Dinner hours usually begin around 6pm with last service at 9 or 10pm. Many restaurants offer an early pre-theatre or 'early bird' dinner up to 7 or 7.30pm, which is usually a good deal. Fixed-price meals are often the best value.

WHERE TO EAT

The choice in Dublin ranges from elegant restaurants, often with French or Modern Irish cuisine, to the humble chip shop offering crispy batter-coated portions of tasty fish and chips (try the famous Leo Burdock's at 2 Werburgh Street, near the Castle). In between, there are pubs, bistros and moderately priced restaurants of all kinds. Dublin's restaurants range from those serving traditional dishes to Chinese, Indian, Japanese, Mongolian, Romanian, Thai, vegetarian cuisine and more.

There are also cafés, self-service snack bars, and the usual fast-food places. Standards of service can vary considerably from one place to the next, but most establishments are welcoming and friendly. Pubs and bars are a good choice for lunch. For our selection of places to eat, see page 106.

Cafés and restaurants in museums, great houses and other attractions are often superior to comparable eateries picking up the traffic outside. They offer everything from pastries and snacks to hot meals with wine. A nice spot is the Irish Film Centre, in the Temple Bar district. Another excellent café-restaurant is in the intimate vaulted basement of the Irish Museum of Modern Art, while the National Gallery museum café (Wintergarden) is also good and stays open until 8pm on Thursday.

A bowl of Irish stew

CAFÉS AND TEAROOMS

While on the streets, Dublin's abandonment of tea in favour of coffee is notable, the Dublin traditional high tea is still going strong in the city's grand hotels, such as the Shelbourne, Westbury and the Gresham. To the background strains of soothing Irish harp or piano music, a liveried waiter will bring you a pot of freshly brewed tea and a silver tray laden with dainty, delicious-looking sandwiches, scones, sweet cakes and pastries.

Dublin is full of cafés where you can get an excellent cup of coffee (and tea if you must) along with a pastry, or a more substantial meal. Cafés also provide some of the best places to sit and watch the world rush by. Still popular is Bewley's Oriental Café on Grafton Street and the tiny but perfect Queen of Tarts on Cork Hill, Dame Street. There are plenty of delicatessens and sandwich bars that cater for the lunch hour trade and many of these are very good indeed.

WHAT TO EAT

STARTERS AND MAIN COURSES

It is no surprise that **fish** and **seafood** figure widely on Dublin menus. Wild Irish salmon tops the list. It can be poached, roasted or steamed, and is generally served simply with light sauces or just a slice of lemon. Alternatively, smoked salmon is a popular choice and is served thinly sliced as a starter or with scrambled eggs as a brunch dish. Cured organic salmon is increasingly seen as a starter at Dublin's finer restaurants.

Dublin Bay prawns are also very popular as a starter. However you choose to eat them, they are always plump, juicy and delicious. Galway Bay oysters are scrumptious – best with a pint of Guinness. A variety of freshwater fish, mussels from Wexford (try the mussel soup), Donegal crab, West Cork King Scallops and Dingle Bay lobster complete the list.

Meat in Irish restaurants is generally served simply to allow the fine flavour to speak for itself. The lamb in Ireland is of the highest quality and features frequently on city menus in guises such as herb-crusted rack of lamb. Irish beef is also a favourite, with prime Irish rib eyes and roasted fillet served with elegant sauces, seasonal vegetables and fondant potatoes. Venison is another popular choice at quality restaurants, as is rabbit or hare. Pork also features strongly, from roast belly of pork to herb-accented gourmet sausages, served simply with mash.

Bewley's Oriental Café

Vegetarians are particularly well catered for in Dublin. There are quite a few specialist and semi-specialist vegetarian places, and often you will have a choice between dishes like vegetable couscous, or parsnips stuffed with brazil nuts and vegetables in a red pepper sauce. Wholesome pasta dishes can be found in Dublin's many Italian restaurants; they are usually a good bet for vegetarian options. Cornucopia on Wicklow Street is strictly vegetarian and serves such a variety of tasty daily specials; you may decide not to eat anywhere else while in the capital.

BREAD, PASTRIES AND DESSERTS
Wonderful freshly baked Irish breads have long been a staple of Dublin cuisine. Unfortunately, the pseudo-croissant is now ubiquitous, but happily so are soda bread, wholemeal bread, and all manner of scrumptious scones. Old-fashioned classic Irish confections like porter cake and barmbrack are also still around.

Whatever your choice of dessert, you will usually be asked if you want cream with it, particularly when served with apple tart. Dessert cakes, puddings, and ice-cream dessert combinations tend to be sweet and rich, so be prepared for a major test of your dietary resolve.

DRINKS

Dublin would not be Dublin without the world-famous stout, Guinness, which really does taste better here than anywhere else. The pouring and settling process takes a little time, but it is worth the wait. Murphy's and other Irish stouts are also wonderful. Don't miss the range of brews now available from microbreweries.

There is also a great array of distinctive Irish whiskeys – you will see their names etched in the glass of pub windows. Wine is readily available everywhere, with a fine selection of Australian cabernets and chardonnays, and Chilean wines. Light Italian reds also feature prominently on wine lists. The cheapest way to order wine is to ask for a carafe of the house wine with your meal. Remember that VAT is charged on wine. It is generally cheaper in Dublin to drink in pubs, rather than hotel bars. Prices are highest in the city centre.

TRADITIONAL FARE

Traditional Irish dishes are now being re-worked for a younger market. Some old-fashioned dishes to look for include colcannon (mashed potatoes with leeks and cabbage), *crubeens* (pigs' trotters), *coddle* (boiled bacon, sausages, onions and potatoes), *boxty* (a tasty potato pancake filled with meat, vegetables or fish), Dublin Lawyer (lobster, flamed in whiskey and simmered in cream) and, of course, the traditional Irish stew, made with lamb, potatoes and vegetables.

PLACES TO EAT

We have used the following symbols to give an idea of the price for an average meal for one, including a service charge of 10–15 percent but excluding wine or other drinks:

€€€€ over 45 euros   **€€** 20–30 euros
€€€ 30–45 euros   **€** below 20 euros

CITY CENTRE SOUTH

Bewley's Grafton Street Café € *78–79 Grafton Street, Dublin 2, tel: 672 7720,* www.bewleys.com. Open Mon–Wed 8am–10pm, Thur–Sat 8am–11pm, Sun 9am–10pm. No-one should miss a trip to the original Bewley's Oriental Café with its art deco windows and paintings. Delicious Fair Trade coffee, teas and a range of dishes are on offer for breakfast, lunch and dinner. Visit the Bewley's Theatre for lunchtime and evening musical and theatrical performances.

Café en Seine € *40 Dawson Street, Dublin 2, tel: 01-677 4567,* www.cafeenseine.ie. Wed–Sat 12pm to 3am, Sun brunch noon–5pm. This is the trendy place to be: stunning Art Deco interior with three-storey atrium featuring intimate bars within bars. The casual, contemporary food is on offer all day and well into the night. The menu is rich with something for every taste, all at prices your pocket will love. For Hors D'Oeuvres try their Warm Crumbed Goats Cheese, Chicken Liver Parfait or Salade Niçoise with home smoked salmon. For lunch try Brioche Du Poulet with Cajun Spices, a homage to French Louisiana.

La Cave €€ *28 South Anne Street, Dublin 2, tel: 679 4409,* www.la cavewinebar.com. Open Mon–Sat 12pm–2am, Sun 5pm–2am. Dublin's oldest authentic French wine bar, with reasonably priced bistro-style dishes. It is decorated with nostalgic posters and prints, and has an excellent wine list plus a late night menu after 11pm. The wine list is extensive with over 350 wines from House to Krug and 40 wines available by the glass, and very good food too. The two-course early bird menu is excellent value for money. When in Dublin this is well worth a visit on a cold or wet day.

The Cedar Tree €€ *11a St Andrew Street, Dublin 2, tel: 677 2121.* Open Mon-Sat 11.30am-11.30pm, Sun 2pm-10pm. The Lebanese food here is authentic and reasonably priced, with good vegetarian options. This truly authentic Lebanese establishment offers wonderful meze dishes, wines and even belly dancers on occasion!

Chili Club €€ *1 Anne's Lane, off South Anne Street, Dublin 2, tel: 677 3721,* www.chiliclub.ie. Open Mon–Fri 12.30–2.30pm and daily 5.30–11pm (Sun to 10pm). One of the oldest Thai restaurants in Dublin. Good, authentic food served in a small, friendly setting. Vegetarian options on an extensive menu.

Cornucopia € *19 Wicklow Street, Dublin 2, tel: 677 7583,* www.cornu copia.ie. Open Mon–Sat 8.30am–9pm, Sun noon–9pm. The food is now better than ever at this favourite vegetarian restaurant. A small, informal place that non-vegetarians can enjoy too. Excellent breakfast spot. They produce delicious home-cooked vegetarian and vegan meals from breakfast through to dinner. Open seven days a week.

South William Bar € *52 South William Street, Dublin 2, tel: 01-677 7007,* www.southwilliam.ie. Daily 2pm-late. Cool, friendly ambience over three floors in the Grafton Street area with an interesting mix of 50s-style American diner and Asian style food – from American ribs to fennel bhaji. Food cooked to order producing vibrant tasty plates.

Dax €€€€ *23 Upper Pembroke Street, Dublin 2, tel: 676 1494,* www.dax.ie. Open Tue–Sat 12.30–10.30pm. Dax is worth visiting for its delightful rustic and continental food with a French emphasis. There is tapas available in the bar.

Dunne & Crescenzi €€ *14–16 South Frederick Street, Dublin 2, tel: 677 3815,* www.dunneandcrescenzi.com. Open Mon–Sat 7.30am–11pm, Sun 10am–10pm. The tables are packed into this small but pleasantly authentic Italian joint, which focuses more on panini and antipasti than on hot dishes. Everything is well prepared and big on taste.

L'Ecrivain €€€€ *109a Lower Baggot Street, Dublin 2, tel: 661 1919,* www.lecrivain.com. Open Mon-Wed and Sat 6.30pm-10pm, Thu-

Fri 12.30pm–10pm. One of the best restaurants in the city, with two Michelin stars for new Irish cuisine prepared with a French accent. It is famous for its fish dishes, using same-day catch from all around Ireland.

Eden €€€ *Meeting House Square, Temple Bar, Dublin 2, tel: 670 537*, www.edenbarandgrill.ie. Open Mon–Fri 12.30–3pm, Sun–Thur 5–10pm, Fri–Sat 6–10pm, Sat–Sun brunch noon–3pm (Sun until 4pm). Serving contemporary food with an Irish twist, Eden has a modern, airy interior with outdoor seating on Meeting House Square.

Fallon & Byrne €€€ *11–17 Exchequer Street, Dublin 2; tel: 472 1000*, www.fallonandbyrne.com. Open Mon–Tue noon–3pm, 6–9pm, Wed–Thur noon–3pm, 6–10pm, Fri–Sat noon–3pm, 6–11pm, Sun noon–4pm. Fallon & Bryne's beautiful dining room makes it a particularly pleasant place to enjoy lunch or Sunday brunch. This French restaurant has good service, quality bistro cooking and a fabulous New York-style deli downstairs – if you have any room left.

Il Fornaio € *IFSC, 1b Valentia House, Custom House Square, Dublin 1, tel: 01-672 1852*, www.ilfornaio.ie. Mon–Fri 9am–10pm, Sat 11am–11pm, Sun 11am–9pm. All day menu. No frills, but there is authentic homemade Italian food at reasonable prices. One of several branches in Dublin, this one located in the up-and-coming financial district. It is fairly small but has outdoor tables to enjoy *al fresco* dining during better weather.

The Fumbally € *Fumbally Lane, Dublin 8, tel: 01-5299 8732*, www.thefumbally.ie, Mon–Fri 8am–5pm, Sat 10am–5pm. The owner-chef co-operative gained experience cooking at festivals and travelling, and the result is a distinctly different eatery, casual and friendly. Local organic and free-range produce is cooked with Middle-eastern and Mediterranean spices.

Good World Chinese Restaurant €€ *18 South Great George's Street, Dublin 2, tel: 677 5373*. Daily 12.30pm–2am. This is a popular place, with the best dim sum in the city. The cooking is good, and less geared to Western tastes than most.

L'Gueuleton €€€ *Fade Street, Dublin 2; tel: 675 3708,* www.lgueule ton.com. Open Mon–Sat12.30–3pm and 6–10pm, Sun 1–4pm, 6–9pm. This rustic yet contemporary French restaurant serves up robust dishes with a classic bistro edge. It is hugely popular and has an undeniable charm with its rickety wooden tables and blackboards. No bookings taken.

Jaipur €€€ *41 South Great Georges Street, Dublin 2, tel: 677 0999.* www.jaipur.ie Daily 5–11pm. Fabulous restaurant serving modern Indian food using Irish ingredients such as organic Wicklow lamb, and with a wine list specially chosen to complement the spicy dishes.

Queen of Tarts € *Cork Hill, Dame Street, Dublin 2, tel: 670 7499.* Mon–Fri8am–7pm, Sat–Sun 9am–7pm. Squeeze yourself into the wonderfully quaint teashop with an array of delectable pastries, cakes and salads to delight your tastebuds. Sisters Yvonne and Regina also have a larger branch around the corner in Cow's Lane.

Restaurant Patrick Guilbaud €€€€ *21 Upper Merrion Street, Dublin 4, tel: 676 4192,* www.restaurantpatrickguilbaud.ie. Tue–Sat 12.30–2.15pm, (Sat opens at 1pm) and 7.30–10.15pm. Set in an elegant 18th-century townhouse adjoining the Merrion Hotel, this is Dublin's finest French restaurant, with prices to match.

The Rustic Stone €€ *17 South Great George's St, Dublin 2, tel: 01-707 9596,* www.rusticstone.ie. Mon–Fri, noon–4.30pm, 5.30pm–10.30pm, Sat 1pm–11pm, Sun, 2pm–9pm. Chef Dylan McGrath prepares the best meat and fish in tasty marinades, and guests cook it themselves at the table on a hot stone. A tempting tapas menu of healthy but indulgent bites, and a 'rustic raw' lunch menu, attract a lively and glam clientele. This is Dublin dining at its liveliest.

Saba €€€ *26–28 Clarendon Street, Dublin 2, tel: 679 2000,* www. sabadublin.com. Mon–Sun noon until 11pm. A popular Thai and Vietnamese eatery, known for its authentic menu and contemporary interior. Wok-based dishes, salads, noodles and curries.

Shanahan's on the Green €€€€ *119 St Stephen's Green, Dublin 2, tel: 01-407 0939,* www.shanahans.ie. Mon–Fri, from 5.30pm, Fri only 12.30–2pm, Sat from 6pm; Sun May–Sept 5.30pm–6.45pm. Luxurious, fashionable and very expensive American steakhouse. The certified Irish Angus beef steaks are magnificent. Good wine list, strong on California.

Steps of Rome €€ *1 Chatham Court, Dublin 2, tel: 670 5630,* www. stepsofrome.ie. Mon–Sat noon–11.30pm, Sun 1pm–10pm. This tiny restaurant has great pizza; the best in Dublin. The service is friendly, and you can take away. Get there early – there are only a few tables. No credit cards and no service charge.

Thornton's Restaurant €€€€ *St Stephen's Green West, Dublin 2, tel: 01-478 7008,* www.thorntonsrestaurant.com. Thur–Sat noon–2pm, Tue–Sat 6–10pm. One Michelin star for one of Dublin's special places. Kevin Thornton is a gifted chef, using fantastic ingredients beautifully presented, with emphasis on flavour, all in deep comfort with impeccable service.

Unicorn 12B €€€€ *12b Merrion Court, off Merrion Row, Dublin 2, tel: 662 4757,* www.unicornrestaurant.com. Mon–Sat 12.30–4.30pm, 6–11pm. Popular with Dublin's media set, the Unicorn comes into its own in the summer when the doors open out onto a pretty courtyard. The regional Italian food is well executed and the huge buffet lunches are a treat.

Yamamori Noodles €€ *71 South Great George's Street, Dublin 2, tel: 475 5001,* www.yamamorinoodles.ie. Daily from 12pm, last orders at 11.30pm. Japanese restaurant and a good choice for noodles. The clientele is predominantly cool.

OLD TOWN/LIBERTIES

JULES €€€€ *74 Dame Street, Dublin 2, tel: 679 4555,* www.very jules.com. Mon–Sat 12.30–2.30pm, and 7–10.30pm. Next to the Olympia Theatre, this small restaurant offers French cuisine in a pleasant, relaxed setting.

Leo Burdock's € *2 Werburgh Street, Dublin 8, tel: 454 0306,* www. leoburdocks.com. Mon–Sat noon–midnight, Sun 4pm–midnight.

Dublin's most famous chippy, established in 1913, has no indoor seating but serves the freshest, most delicious fish and chips to take away. Opposite Christchurch Cathedral.

TEMPLE BAR

Elephant and Castle €€ *19 Temple Bar, Dublin 2, tel: 679 3121*, www.elephantandcastle.ie. Mon–Fri 8.30am–11.30pm, Sat–Sun 10.30am–11.30pm. Good food and reasonable prices have assured the continuing popularity of this informal place. Come here for burgers and salads as well as the famous spicy chicken wings.

Gallagher's Boxty House €€ *20–21 Temple Bar, Dublin 2, tel: 677 2762*, www.boxtyhouse.ie. Daily noon-10.30pm, Sat from 9am. Boxty is an old Irish dish: potato pancakes stuffed with a variety of fillings (including vegetarian), served at long tables to traditional Irish background music; a must stop for every tourist.

CITY CENTRE NORTH

Chapter One Restaurant €€€€ *18–19 Parnell Square, Dublin 1, tel: 873 2266*, www.chapteronerestaurant.com. Tue–Fri 12.30–2pm, Tue–Sat 6–10.30pm. One of the city's best restaurants, set in the basement of the Dublin Writers Museum, with excellent modern Irish dishes accompanied by fine wines.

Ely Gastropub €€ *Grand Canal Square, Dublin 2 tel: 633 9986*, www.elywinebar.ie. Daily noon–10pm, later on Fri and Sat. Clearly aimed at the young crowd, in the up-and-coming Dockland area, this gastro pub serves good organic food, a wide range of beers and great wine.

Gallery Restaurant at the Church €€ *Mary Street, Dublin 1, tel: 828 0102*, www.thechurch.ie. 5–10pm or later. This is a stunning venue that comes complete with a massive church organ and stained-glass windows. An international menu with an Irish twist is served.

SOUTH SUBURBS

The Lobster Pot €€€€ *9 Ballsbridge Terrace, Dublin 4, tel: 668 0025,* www.thelobsterpot.ie. Mon–Fri noon–2pm, 6–10.30pm, Sat 6–10.30pm. This restaurant has a charming, old-world atmosphere and an exquisite fish menu. Choose from the daily catch and have it cooked to your liking.

Roly's Bistro €€€ *7 Ballsbridge Terrace, Dublin 4, tel: 668 0623,* www.rolysbistro.ie. Noon–3pm and 5.45–10pm. Attractive bistro restaurant on two floors, with imaginative and well-presented menus, usually focused on classic fish and meat dishes. Good service and a lively atmosphere.

OUTSIDE DUBLIN

Caviston's €€€ *59 Glasthule Road, Sandycove, County Dublin, tel: 280 9245,* www.cavistons.com. Tue–Sat, lunch is over three sittings: noon–1.30pm, 1.30–3pm and 3–5pm; Fri–Sat, dinner is over two sittings: 6–8.15pm, 8.15pm–close. This tiny fish-restaurant has gained an excellent reputation for the freshest fish.

King Sitric €€€€ *East Pier, Howth, Co. Dublin, tel: 01-832 5235,* www.kingsitric.ie. Thur–Sat, 6.30–10pm, Sun1–5pm & 6.30–10pm. A long-established fine-dining restaurant in a lovely waterside setting. Chef/patron Aidan McManus is committed to fish fresh from the boats (or his own lobster pots) and has a fine wine list. The East Café Bar (€) is open for light bites (tapas-style menu) from 10.30am Wed–Sun.

Nautilus €€ *Marine Court, The Green, Malahide, Co Dublin, tel: 01-845 1233.* Mon–Fri from 5pm, Sat–Sun 1pm–late. Elegant and relaxed dining atmosphere in an elevated room overlooking Malahide Marina. Beautifully presented plates of local seafood and Irish meat dishes served by friendly, efficient staff. Try the Seafood Platter.

A–Z TRAVEL TIPS

A Summary of Practical Information

A

ACCOMMODATION (See also Youth Hostels)

Hotels in Ireland are classified by star ratings from one to five stars, and are registered and regularly inspected by the Irish Tourist Board (Bord Fáilte). The Tourist Board also publishes a list of approved hotel and guesthouse accommodation throughout Dublin, obtainable through your local tourist information office (see Tourist Information). Hotel information can also be found on the Irish Hotels Federation website www.irelandhotels.com. All tourism information offices operate an accommodation reservation service. It is always advisable to book accommodation in advance, especially if you plan to visit in the peak months of July and August.

Hotels generally offer a full range of services, including restaurants, licensed bars, currency exchange offices, gift shops and lounges, while **guesthouses** provide more limited facilities, but are excellent value. Be aware that room prices quoted normally include the government tax (VAT) of 9 percent but do not always include service charges, which could add an extra 10 to 15 percent to your bill.

Details about **self-catering accommodation** in Dublin and the surrounding area can be obtained from the Irish Tourist Board, which produces a complete illustrated guide. Dublin also offers a variety of college and **university accommodation** when classes are not being held. Rooms and apartments at bargain rates are available on the Trinity College campus between mid-June and mid-September. For further information, contact the Accommodation Office, Trinity College, Dublin 2, tel :01 896 1177, www.tcd.ie. University College Dublin provides a similar service. For further information, contact Accommodation Office, UCD, Belfield, Dublin 4, tel: 01 716 1034, www.ucd. ie. Details of student accommodation can be obtained from USIT, 19 Aston Quay, Dublin 2, tel: 01 609 1906, www.usit.ie.

Holiday Hostels provide simple accommodation in dormitory-style rooms or shared bedrooms for visitors on a tight budget and are open all year. For details of hostels in Dublin, contact the Irish Tourist Board. Three places you can contact directly are:

Avalon House, Budget Accommodation Centre, 55 Aungier Street, Dublin 2, tel: 01 475 0001, www.avalon-house.ie.

Kinlay House Dublin, Accommodation Centre, 2–12 Lord Edward Street, Dublin 2, tel: 01 679 6644, www.kinlayhouse.ie.

Independent Holiday Hostels, tel:01 215 8786, www.hostels-ireland.com.

AIRPORTS

Dublin International Airport (tel: 01 814 1111; www.dublinairport. com) is 11km (7 miles) north of the city centre. Buses and taxis service the airport. **Airlink** (Nos 747 and 748; www.dublinbus.ie) is a regular shuttle service connecting to the city centre, operated by Dublin Bus. Buses leave from outside the Arrivals Hall and connect with the central bus station (Busáras), railway stations (Heuston Station, Connolly Rail/DART station) and the city centre. Buses leave every 10–15 minutes from 5.45am until 11.30pm. You can buy your tickets from the bus driver. If you are spending a few days in Dublin you may save money by buying Dublin Bus day tickets from the information counter in the Arrivals Hall: the airport transfer by Dublin Bus is included in the ticket. **Aircoach** (www.aircoach.ie) operates a competing 24-hour service with buses leaving every 10 minutes from 6am–8pm and less frequently after that. A cheaper option, if you have plenty of time, is to take city buses 16A, 41, 46x or 746 to the city centre.

B

BICYCLE RENTAL

There are 450 bikes for hire from 40 bike stations throughout the city centre (www.dublinbikes.ie). You can download information of routes and maps from a number of organisations: The Dublin Cycle Campaign (www.dublincycling.com) has been working for improved conditions for cyclists in the city; while Dublin City Council (www.

dublincitycycling.ie) is encouraging cycling and improving safety.

You can also hire bikes from: Neill's Wheels (55 Aungier Street, www.rentabikedublin.com), Belfield Bike Shop (N11 gate of University College Dublin, www.belfieldbikeshop.com, tel: 01 716 1697), Phoenix Park Bike Hire (Chesterfield Avenue gate entrance into Phoenix Park; tel: 01 87 379 9946; www.phoenixparkbikehire.com) and Cycleways Ltd (Parnell Street; tel: 01 873 4748; www.cycle ways.com). Cycling Safaris (Belfield Bike Shop, university campus UCD, Dublin 4, tel: 01 260 0749; www.cyclingsafaris.com) offer both guided and self-guided day trips in and around Dublin.

BUDGETING FOR YOUR TRIP

Dublin is relatively expensive compared to other European capitals, and accommodation and eating out can quickly eat into your budget. The following is a rough guide only:

Accommodation. A double room in a mid-range hotel in Dublin costs from about €100 upwards per room, but you will find most places hovering around the €150 mark. Five-star hotels can easily set you back three or four times this amount. There are plenty of inexpensive accommodation options if you are prepared to look around.

Meals and drinks. Stopping off for a coffee in Dublin can often be expensive at around €2.50 to €3 for a cappuccino or latte. Drinks in bars and pubs are expensive and nowhere more so than in hotels. In city centre pubs you will pay around €5 for a pint of lager, while a spirit and a mixer can set you back around €7. Guinness usually costs from around €4.50 a pint. Most restaurants are mid-range with main courses around €20 and upwards.

Entertainment. Cinema tickets costs around €10 depending on location, time and any discounts you may be entitled to; admission to a nightclub is usually upward of €10. Many museums and galleries have free admission making sightseeing a relatively cheap option.

Transport. A full day bus ticket for an adult costs €6.90, including airport transfer; bus/Luas (tram) inner city day ticket costs €8.10

and bus/rail/Luas costs €12. A three-day unlimited travel ticket costs €28 for bus, rail and Luas. See www.dublinbus.ie.

Specials: The Dublin Pass ticket (www.dublinpass.ie) includes free entry to over 30 top visitor attractions; discounts at shops, restaurants, cafés, theatres, venues, tours; free transport to Dublin City with Aircoach from the airport; and an 86 page guidebook to Dublin. Dublin passes are available for 1, 2, 3 and 5 days. Prices start at €49 for an adult day pass.

C

CAR HIRE (See also Driving)

Driving in the city is difficult, but it is worth hiring a car to explore the surrounding countryside. You can arrange to hire a car immediately upon arrival the airport, or have one waiting for you if you book a fly-drive or rail-sail-drive inclusive package. To hire a car you will need a driving licence issued in your home country, valid for at least two to five years. The minimum age (usually 23–25 years) varies from company to company, and most do not rent to over-70 or 75s. Rates include third-party liability insurance, and sometimes collision damage waiver (CDW) but check for excess liabilities. The cost of hiring a medium-sized car for one day in Dublin can range from as little as €12 in February to €100 in August.

Major car hire companies:

Avis, Airport Arrivals Hall and 35–39 Old Kilmainham Road, Dublin 8, tel: 01 605 7500, www.avis.ie.

Budget, Airport Arrivals Hall and 151 Drumcondra Road Lower, Dublin 9, tel: 01 844 5150 (airport), 01 837 9611, www.budget.ie.

Hertz, Airport Arrivals Hall, tel: 01 844 5466, www.hertz.ie.

National, Airport Arrivals Hall and 29 Parkgate Street (serviced by Europcar), Dublin 4, tel: 01 260 3771, www.nationalcar.com.

Argus, a local company, is at the airport and other city locations, tel: 01 843 5787, www.arguscarhire.com.

Dan Dooley, another local company, is at the Airport Arrivals Hall and Westland Row, city centre, tel: 01 677 2723, www.dan-dooley.ie.

CLIMATE

Dublin's has a temperate climate without extremes of temperature, thanks to the warming Gulf Stream that influences much of the country. The weather is unpredictable and can change very quickly from rain to sun (and vice versa) due to blustery winds coming in from the Irish Sea. However, less rain falls on Dublin than on any other part of the country and snow is a rare occurrence. Summers can be quite cool and days can be unexpectedly warm in winter.

	J	F	M	A	M	J	J	A	S	O	N	D
°C	7	8	11	13	16	18	20	21	17	14	11	8
°F	45	46	52	55	61	64	68	70	63	57	52	46

CLOTHING

Dubliners are fashion-conscious, and a certain standard of attire is expected in exclusive hotels and restaurants. Business people still dress in formal dark suits. For everyday wear, however, jeans and casual clothes are appropriate. A raincoat or umbrella is an absolute necessity. If you plan to walk a lot, especially in the environs, bring sturdy shoes and a sweater: even if it looks like a glorious day, it can turn cold later on. Pack warm clothing for winter, and a jacket and sweater in summer. Evening temperatures on the sunniest summer days can be quite cool; in spring there is often a chilling wind that adds an edge to the day's mild warmth.

CRIME AND SAFETY (See also Emergencies)

Compared to most urban centres, Dublin's crime rate is moderate, and violent street crime is rare. Unfortunately, crime is on the increase. Be wary of pickpockets in pubs or crowded places.

Avoid Phoenix Park after dark.

If you are robbed, report the incident to the hotel receptionist and the nearest police station so that the police can provide you with a certificate to present to your insurance company. Call your consulate if your passport has been stolen. Tourist information offices and some attractions provide a multilingual leaflet produced by the Garda (see Police), entitled *A Short Guide to Tourist Security*. The Irish Tourist Assistance Service (www.itas.ie) is there to help tourists who fall victim to crime. Opening hours are Mon–Fri 10am–6pm (6–7 Hanover Street East, Dublin 2; tel: 1890 365 700 / 01 661 0562); Sat, Sun and holidays (Garda Station, Store Street; tel: 01 666 8109).

D

DRIVING

Road Conditions. If you must drive in the city centre, avoid the worst congestion by travelling between 10am and 4pm. Outside the city, the motorway system offers rapid transit. However the most scenic routes, such as those through the Wicklow Mountains, tend to be narrow, winding and steep.

Rules and Regulations. Traffic follows the same basic rules that apply in Britain. Drive on the left and overtake on the right. Turn left on a roundabout; at a junction where no road has priority, yield to traffic coming from the right. Road signs giving place directions are bilingual, in Irish and English, and distances are shown in kilometres. Seat belts in both the front and back must be worn, and children under-12 must travel in the rear. Ireland has very strict rules about drinking and driving – don't do it.

Petrol (gas). There are filling stations everywhere, many of them open 24 hours. Petrol is dispensed from the green-handled nozzle: the black one is diesel.

Parking. It is almost impossible to find free parking on Dublin's streets during normal working hours, but you may have better luck at weekends. Expect to be towed away or heavily fined for parking illegally. Metered parking (for up to 2 hours) is quite limited. Your safest bet is to park in one of the multistorey car parks, which are not expensive.

Speed limits. The speed limit is 50kph in towns and cities, 80kph on regional and local roads and 100kph on national roads. On motorways the speed limit is 120kph.

If You Need Help. If you are a member of an AIT driving club or the AA, call the Automobile Association of Ireland (tel: 01 617 9999 or emergency 1800 66 77 88). The Royal Automobile Club (RAC) also has a breakdown number (toll-free: 1800 535005).

E

ELECTRICITY

Ireland's electrical supply is 220 volts 50 cycles AC. Plugs are 3-pin flat or 2-pin round. If you need a travel adaptor, bring one with you.

EMBASSIES AND CONSULATES

Australia: Fitzwilton House, Wilton Terrace, Dublin 2, tel: 01 664 5300, www.ireland.embassy.gov.au

Canada: 7–8 Wilton Terrace, Dublin 2, tel: 01 234 4000, www.canada.ie

South Africa: Earlsfort Centre, Dublin 2, tel: 01 661 5553, www.embassy-dublin.com/south-africa.html

UK: 29 Merrion Road, Dublin 4, tel: 01 205 3700, www.british embassy.ie

US: 42 Elgin Road, Dublin 4, tel: 01 668 8777, http://dublin.us embassy.gov/

EMERGENCIES (See also Health and Medical Care and Police)

In the event of an emergency, dial 999 or 112 for Police, Ambulance, Fire and Coastguard. The call is free from all pay and card phones.

G

GAY AND LESBIAN TRAVELLERS

The gay and lesbian community is both visible and welcoming to visitors. The monthly newspaper, *Gay Community News* (www.gcn.ie) is widely available, and there are listings and features in many of Dublin's free magazines and papers. Annual gay events include the Dublin Gay Theatre Festival (May), Pride (late June), and the Lesbian and Gay Film Festival (in the Irish Film Centre, end of July). Good bars and nightclubs include the long-standing George (South Great George's Street), The Front Lounge (Parliament Street) and Dragon (South Great George's Street).

Help and information lines include Gay Switchboard Dublin (tel: 01 872 1055; www.gayswitchboard.ie) and Lesbian Line (tel: 01 872 9911; www.dublinlesbianline.ie). Outhouse (105 Capel Street, Dublin 2; tel: 01 873 4932; www.outhouse.ie) is a meeting place for the lesbian and gay community.

GETTING THERE (See also Airports)

By Air. Ireland's national airline is Aer Lingus www.aerlingus.com, which operates direct flights to Dublin from Birmingham, Edinburgh, Gatwick, Glasgow, London Heathrow and Manchester in the UK. Major air connections from the Continent include Amsterdam, Berlin, Brussels, Frankfurt, Geneva, Madrid, Munich, Paris, Prague, Rome/da Vinci, Vienna and Warsaw. Ireland's other national airline, Ryanair www.ryanair.com operates budget flights to Dublin from London Gatwick/Luton/Stansted, Aberdeen, Belfast City, Birmingham, Bristol, Doncaster, Durham, Edinburgh, East Midlands, Glasgow Prestwick, Leeds, Liverpool, Manchester and Newcastle.

Visitors flying from Australia, Canada or New Zealand must make connections through London or another British hub with Aer Lingus, British Airways, British Midlands or Ryanair. Connections can also be made through another European hub: Air France, Lufthansa and SAS fly to Dublin. Packages that include a hotel room generally offer the best rates and conditions. A wide range of package tours or special-interest holidays is available, including fly-drive, sporting and activity holidays, and short breaks.

By Bus. Bus services linking Britain and Dublin are operated by Bus Éireann (www.buseireann.ie), Ireland's national bus company (Travel Centre, Busáras, Store Street, Dublin 1; tel: 01 836 6111), in conjunction with Eurolines via Dublin Ferryport and with Stena Line or Irish Ferries via Dun Laoghaire. Routes connect London and other major British towns to Dublin's central bus station, Busáras.

Countrywide bus services throughout Ireland are also provided by Bus Éireann. Departures are from Busáras (the central bus station), located in Store Street.

By Ferry. There are two main ferry companies. Irish Ferries runs ships from Dublin Port to Holyhead (tel: 0818 300 400 for information and reservations in Ireland; 08717 300 200 in the UK; www.irishferries.com). Stena Line (reservations and information in Ireland; tel: 01 204 7777; in the UK tel: 0844 770 7070; www.stenaline.co.uk) operates boats from the Ferry Terminal in Dun Laoghaire to Holyhead. They offer both a regular service and a high-speed service that takes about half the normal time. Irish Ferries also sails from Rosslare to Roscoff and Cherbourg.

GUIDED TOURS

Bus Tours. City sightseeing tours by bus provide an excellent introduction to Dublin. Dublin Bus (59 Upper O'Connell Street, Dublin 1; tel: 01 703 3028; www.dublinsightseeing.ie) operates a city tour that takes in the principal sights; in good weather, the tour is by open-top bus. The bus-driving tour guides are entertaining, sometimes there is a sing-song, you can hop on or off at any of the stops, and your ticket is valid all day. Irish City Tours (tel: 01 605 7705; www.irishcitytours.com) has a similar service, with tickets available on the bus. Dublin Bus also has an amusing, offbeat Ghost Bus Tour in the evening.

Bus Éireann runs day trips out of the city to sights such as Glendalough, Newgrange and the Boyne Valley, Wicklow and Powerscourt Gardens, as well as further afield. All tours depart from the Travel Centre at Busáras (see page 122). Gray Line Tours (17 Upper O'Connell Street, Dublin 1; tel: 01 605 7705; www.grayline.com) offers a similar range of excursions. Tours depart from the O'Connell Street office next door to Clery's Department Store.

Walking Tours. Dublin Tourism's Rock'n'Stroll Trail for music fans, points out places associated with such artists as Bob Geldof, U2, Sinead O'Connor and the Chieftains, among others. Dublin Tourism also has The Visit Dublin Official Mobile App Guide, a free download for Smartphones. It covers different themes including Viking and Medieval Dublin, Georgian Dublin, Temple Bar to Docklands and the Historic Northside.

The enjoyable Dublin Literary Pub Crawl comprises an evening of readings, song and performance following in the footsteps of James Joyce, Samuel Beckett, Brendan Behan and others (tel: 670 5602; www.dublinpubcrawl.com, or book at the Dublin Tourism Centre). Historical Walking Tours of Dublin have walks on various themes from architecture to Vikings (tel: 087 688 9412; www.historicaltours.ie). The Traditional Irish Musical Pub Crawl is led by a couple of professional musicians – they play and sing, and talk about the history of Irish music. You can book at the Tourism Centre or contact Discover Dublin (tel: 01 475 3313; www.discoverdublin.ie).

Pat Liddy's walking tours can be booked at the Dublin Bus Office (59 Upper O'Connell Street), or at the Tours & Tickets Office opposite the main gate of Trinity College (tel: 01 832 9406; www.walkingtours.ie). The tours cover the highlights of Dublin's literary locations and Georgian architecture.

The International Bar on Wicklow Street is the starting point for the daily 1916 Rebellion Walking Tour taking in sights of the Easter Rising (tel: 086 8 583 847; www.1916rising.com).

Join the excellent, free Sandemans tour (www.newdublintours.

com) leaving from City Hall at 11am and 1pm for a three-hour tips-only jaunt around. Food enthusiasts can take an enjoyable stroll through the historic centre tracing the origins of Irish food and how it has shaped Irish society (meet at Trinity College every Sat at 11.30am; tel: 087 688 9412; www.historicalinsights.ie).

Wet and Dry Tour. Viking Splash Tours (tel: 707 6000; www.viking splash.ie) depart from St Stephen's Green North in a vehicle that takes you along the canals and rivers of Dublin, as well as the streets.

H

HEALTH AND MEDICAL CARE

Visitors who are not covered by their medical insurance should take out a short-term holiday policy before setting out. Citizens of EU countries are covered by a reciprocal agreement and may use the Irish health services for medical treatment and hospital stays. However, repatriation costs are not covered. British visitors should make sure they have a European Health Insurance Card (EHIC), available from post offices or online.

In the event of an accident, dial 999 or 112 for an ambulance. Your hotel or guesthouse proprietor will contact a doctor in an emergency. Beaumont Hospital (Beaumont Road, Dublin 9; tel: 809 3000) has a 24-hour emergency room. For non-emergency services, try the Grafton Street Medical Centre (Grafton Street; tel: 01 671 2122).

If you need emergency dental treatment, call the Irish Dental Association (Unit 2, Leopardstown Office Park, Sandyford, Dublin 8; tel: 01 295 0072; www.dentist.ie), which will be able to recommend a dentist.

Pharmacies are generally open during normal business hours. You can find the address of the nearest late-night pharmacy in the local press and under 'Chemists – Pharmaceutical' in the phone directory. There is a branch of Boots Chemists on Grafton Street. Chemists on O'Connell Street tend to stay open quite late.

HOLIDAYS

Shops, banks, official departments and restaurants are closed on public holidays. If a holiday falls on a Sunday, the following Monday is normally taken instead. Although Good Friday is not officially a public holiday, it is observed as such in most of Ireland and pubs are closed on that day.

1 January: New Year's Day
17 March: St Patrick's Day
25 December: Christmas Day
26 December: St Stephen's Day
Movable Dates
March/April: Good Friday/Easter Monday
First Monday in June: Whit or June Holiday
First Monday in August: Summer Bank Holiday
Last Monday in October: All Souls

LANGUAGE

Ireland is officially bilingual, and on official occasions either English or Irish may be used. English is spoken in Dublin and throughout most of Ireland; Irish is the main language in the areas designated as *Gaeltacht*. However, Irish is a required school subject, so most Irish people have knowledge of it. Signs around Dublin are usually self-explanatory. On buses, An *Lár* means 'City Centre.'

MAPS

For detailed maps of Dublin and the area around it, try the Dublin *Street Atlas and Guide* (available in bookstores), or buy a similar mini-atlas. If you need less detail, the tourism office gives away free copies of *The Dublin Map*: useful as all attractions are plotted on it.

MEDIA

Radio and TV. The national broadcasting authority is RTE (*Radio Telefís Éireann*) which runs several TV channels, RTE1 and RTE2, and three radio stations, RTE1, 2FM, and Lyric FM. TG4 is a television station with programmes in Irish. There are also two independent stations, TV3 and 3e. Television programmes from Britain via the BBC and ITV (independent television) are available, as well as all the BBC radio stations. Many hotels are equipped to receive satellite television or cable via Sky TV and other operators.

Newspapers and Magazines. The *Irish Times* is the leading national daily, with interesting articles and a useful Notices section. The *Irish Independent* has more Ireland focused coverage and publishes a special Sunday edition. The *Evening Herald*, hawked at numerous street corners, is Dublin's local tabloid, with an extensive Classifieds section. In the morning, watch out for Herald AM and Metro, which are given out free at DART stations. Most newsagents stock the main UK national dailies, plus the Irish edition of London's *Sunday Times*, and many sell American and European newspapers. Foreign newspapers and periodicals can be purchased at Easons, located at 40–42 Lower O'Connell Street.

For what's going on, try *Totally Dublin*, an events listings magazine. For news of pop ups, street markets and other cutting-edge events see the online magazine, http://dublin.lecool.com.

MONEY

Currency. Ireland's monetary unit is the euro (€), which is divided into 100 cent (¢). Banknotes are issued in €5, €10, €20, €50, €100 and also €500 denominations. Coins come in 1, 2, 5, 10, 20 and 50 cents and 1 and 2 euro.

Changing money. For the best exchange rate, visitors should use banks, post offices and bureaux de change. The best rates are often obtained by using a credit card. Note that the Bank of Ireland ATMs charge for transactions with foreign banks.

Credit cards and travellers' cheques. Credit/debit cards are accepted in most hotels, restaurants, petrol stations and large shops. Some guesthouses may not accept credit cards, so be sure to ask before booking. Travellers' cheques, supported by identification, can be exchanged at most banks or main travel service offices.

O

OPENING HOURS

Banks are usually open 10am–4pm Monday–Friday and 10am–5pm on Thursday; nearly all are open at lunchtime. Later closing times are gradually being introduced throughout Ireland.

Some shops follow Dublin's normal opening hours: Monday–Saturday 9/9.30am–5.30/6pm, with late night shopping on Thursday until 8pm. A few suburban shopping centres stay open until 9pm on Thursday or Friday. In tourist areas hours are usually extended, and most places in Grafton Street remain open well into the evening and on Sunday.

Most pubs are open all day from 10.30am to 12.30am, with a slightly later opening on Sunday, and earlier closing in winter. Many pubs in the city centre stay open until 1.30am or later from Thursday to Saturday.

P

POLICE

The emergency number for the Garda is 999 or 112. Garda Headquarters is at Harcourt Square, Dublin 2; tel: 01 666 6666.

POST OFFICES

Post office branches are open Monday–Friday 9am–5.30pm, and Saturday 9am–1pm. There is a post office at Dublin Airport, a convenient branch is near the tourist office on St Andrew Street and a branch on

Merrion Row close to the museums and St Stephen's Green. Mailboxes are painted green and have the word 'Post' in yellow on the top.

Dublin's main post office is the General Post Office (GPO) in O'Connell Street. It is open 8am–6pm Monday–Saturday. Many post offices exchange foreign currency and travellers' cheques.

PUBLIC TRANSPORT

Bus. Dublin Bus (Bus Átha Cliath) operates the city's bus network. The company is a subsidiary of the national transport company, CIE. The head office is at 59 O'Connell Street, Dublin 1 (tel: 01 873 4222; www.dublinbus.ie). Their yellow and blue single and double deckers serve the city and the Greater Dublin area. Buses run from 6am–11.30pm. On popular routes, buses run every 10–20 minutes, but service on other routes could be much less frequent. There is a special half-hourly Nitelink service to the suburbs from midnight–4am Friday and Saturday (buses depart from College, D'Olier and Westmoreland streets every half hour; buy your tickets in advance at the stops or pay on the bus with coins only; €5). A frequent bus service links Heuston Station and Busáras with Dublin airport. You need to have the right change ready unless you have a special pass (see below), which should be inserted into the reader as you enter the bus on the right hand side (combined bus/DART tickets should be shown to the driver/conductor). If you over-pay, the driver will print you a credit slip. Collect these and they will refund your money at the headquarters on O'Connell Street.

Fares. There are no flat fares on public transport, and the amount you pay depends on where you want to go. For €5 you can buy a Leap card (www.leapcard.ie), and top it up in multiples of €5, using it to pay your fare to the bus driver (it is not a swipe card), avoiding the need to carry a stash of small change. It can also be used on the Luas tram. A range of discount passes is available for bus or combined bus-and rail. The one-day adult bus ticket allows unlimited travel on all Dublin Bus services, except Nitelink. The one-day and three-day short-hop bus/rail tickets allow unlimited transport on Dublin Bus and DART for one person (except on Nitelink), while the family one-day ticket extends the same concessions to two adults and up to four children under 16. Combination bus and Luas tram tickets are also available. Seven-day passes are also available for unlimited travel on the bus, including the Airlink service. There are also a variety of student and children's passes. Passes can be obtained from the Dublin Bus booking office at 59 O'Connell Street, or from any bus ticket agent.

Luas Tram. The Luas tram (tel: 1800 300 604 toll-free in Ireland; www.luas.ie) is Dublin's Light Rail Transit system, connecting the city centre with outlying suburbs. There are two lines that operate weekdays 5.30am–12.30am, Sat 6.30am–12.30am, Sun 7am–11.30pm. The Red Line runs from The Point to Tallaght every 10–12 minutes, with stops at Connolly Station, Four Courts, Smithfield, the National Museum and Heuston Station. The Green Line runs from St Stephen's Green to Sandyford every 5–15 minutes. Single fares range from €1.60 to €3.10 depending on the distance travelled. All stops have ticket machines. Return tickets, one-day and seven-day tickets are also available.

Rail/DART. Dublin Area Rapid Transit (DART) provides a swift and efficient electrified rail link through the city, from the seaside towns of Howth and Malahide in the north and Greystones in the south. The line runs along the Dublin Bay coast and serves a total of 30 stations. Trains run approximately every 15 minutes (every 5 minutes during rush hours) 5.30am–midnight Monday–Saturday, and 9am–11.30pm Sunday. Avoid travelling at peak times when trains are packed with commuters. Single fares range from €1.70 to €4.35.

Taxi. You'll find taxis at one of the many clearly marked taxi ranks located outside major hotels, bus and railway stations, and on busy thoroughfares. Taxis do not normally cruise for business. There are 24-hour taxi ranks at Aston Quay, College Green, O'Connell Street, Eden Quay, Grafton Street Lower and St Stephen's Green (North). At busy times there can be a long wait. You can also order a taxi by calling a specific company; look in the Golden Pages of the telephone directory under 'Taxicabs'.

Rates are fixed by law and displayed in all taxis. See www.transportforireland.ie for a fare estimator. They are valid for a 16km (10-mile) radius outside the city; beyond that, fares should be negotiated in advance with the driver.

T

TELEPHONES

The dialling code for the Dublin area when calling from outside the city is 01; the code for Ireland is 353. Direct-dial local and international calls can be made from all hotels and most guesthouses or from any public phone. Bear in mind that any calls made from a hotel will have a hefty surcharge.

To make a call within Dublin, dial only the seven-digit number. To call Dublin from elsewhere in Ireland, dial the 01 area code plus the seven-digit number. The access number for international calls is 00, followed by the country code. Pay-phone international calls are cheaper after 6pm Mon–Fri and at any time over the weekend. Though there are still some coin phones, telephone calling cards are widely used; you can buy them in units of 10, 20, 50 or 100 from post offices, newsstands or shops displaying a phone card notice.

For mobile (cell) phones you will need a GSM celluar phone in Ireland. It is possible to rent these but this is an expensive option unless you anticipate a long stay. If you have a GSM phone the roaming charges may well be high. The cheapest option is to buy a local Ireland SIM card for your phone; incoming calls will be free and local calls inexpensive. Your phone must be unlocked by your carrier for this to work. Check out all the options before travelling.

For directory enquires for Ireland and Northern Ireland dial 11811. For UK and International dial 11818. Operators can be accessed through the numbers above.

TIME ZONES

Ireland follows Greenwich Mean Time (GMT: 1 hour earlier than Central European Time) from November to March and summer time (the same as Britain) from April to October. Ireland's latitude means that summer days are long (it's light until around 11pm), and that daylight hours in mid-winter are quite short (it's dark by 3.30pm).

New York	**Dublin**	Paris	Jo'burg	Sydney
7am	**noon**	1pm	2pm	10pm

TIPPING

Hotel bills usually include a service charge. If a service charge is included in a restaurant bill, tipping is not obligatory. If you are unsure whether a service charge has been added, ask; if not, give 10–12 percent. Give your hairdresser/barber about 10–12 percent; porters €1–2 per bag; taxi drivers 10–12 percent.

TOILETS

Dublin is not well provided with public conveniences. Around Grafton Street, the shopping centres and Marks & Spencer have toilets on their top floors; there are toilets downstairs in the Trinity College Arts Building inside the Nassau Street gate. Use the facilities in museums, department stores or pubs. Toilets may be labelled with symbols, or with the words *Fir* for men and *Mná* for women.

TOURIST INFORMATION

Irish Tourist Board (Fáilte Ireland)

General enquiries: Fáilte Ireland, 88–95, Amiens Street Dublin 1; tel: 01-884 7700; (0808-234 2009 in UK, in Ireland 1800 363 626); www.ireland.com.

Within the Republic visit www.discoverireland.ie. For tourist information within Ireland tel. 1890 324 583.

Dublin City: Dublin Tourism, Suffolk Street, (near Grafton Street) Dublin 2; tel: 01-605 7700 (0800-039 7000 in UK); www.visitdublin.com.

Tourism Ireland Offices Abroad

Australia: 36 Carrington Street, Sydney NSW 2000; tel: 02-9299 6177; www.ireland.com

Canada: 2 Bloor Street West, Suite 3403, Toronto, Ontario M4W 3E2; tel: 800 223 6470 or 416-925 6368; www.ireland.com

New Zealand: Level 6, 18 Shortland Street, Private Bag 92136, Auckland 1; tel: +649-977 2255; www.ireland.com

UK: Nations House, 103 Wigmore Street, London W1U 1QS; tel: 020-7518 0800; www.ireland.com

US: 345 Park Avenue, New York, NY 10154; tel: 212-418 0800 or 1800-SHAMROCK; www.ireland.com

The **Dublin Tourism Centre** (Suffolk Street, Dublin 2; tel: 884 7700; www.visitdublin.com) is located in the renovated St Andrew's church. They have information desks and can book tours, theatre and concert tickets, and accommodation (for a small charge), and have a wealth of brochures and other information. The centre is open all year Mon–Sat 9am–5.30pm (until 7pm July–Aug) Sun 10.30am–3pm.

Other locations are at the following addresses: Arrivals Building, Dublin Airport (daily 8am–10pm); 14 Upper O'Connell Street, Dublin 2 (Mon–Sat 9am–5pm); Dun Laoghaire Ferry Terminal (Mon–Fri 9.30am–1.15pm, 2.30–5.30pm).

TRAVELLERS WITH DISABILITIES

Some historic buildings and museums do not provide wheelchair access. A facilities and accessibility guide and fact sheets can be obtained for free from the Irish Tourist Board. Other useful contacts are the National Disability Authority (tel: 01 608 0400; www.nda.ie) and the Irish Wheelchair Association (tel: 01 818 6400; www.iwa.ie).

V

VISAS

For a stay of up to three months in Ireland, a valid passport is sufficient for citizens of Australia, Canada, New Zealand, South Africa and the US. Visitors from European Union (EU) countries need only bring an identity card and are free to stay indefinitely in the country, and work if they wish.

W

WEBSITES AND INTERNET ACCESS

Information on the web can help you get ready for your trip to Dublin. You can make hotel guesthouse or B&B reservations at www.goireland.com or www.visitdublin.com. The Irish Hotels Federation has a site at www.irelandhotels.com, and B&Bs can be booked at www.irelandbnb.com.

For sightseeing and other general information: www.ireland.com is the official marketing website of the Irish Tourist Board and will help you to plan your holiday. Dublin Tourism's site is www.visitdublin.com. Dúchas, the Heritage Services, also has a site: www.heritageireland.ie. To see what's going on try www.entertainmentireland.ie. Free Wi-Fi access is available in many cafes, and most hotels offer guests free internet access. Most hotels and hostels have a computer available for guests to access the internet. Kiosks at Dublin airport offer access. The Global Internet Cafe is centrally located on O'Connell Street.

Y

YOUTH HOSTELS

Independent Holiday Hostels of Ireland operates 9 hostels in Dublin and over 100 throughout the country. The headquarters are at P.O. Box 11772, Fairview, Dublin 3; tel: 01-836 4700; www.hostels-ireland.com.

RECOMMENDED HOTELS

There is often little difference between hotels and guesthouses in Dublin, but the latter are usually cheaper, while city centre hotels, especially in Temple Bar, tend to be noisier.

Listed below is a selection of hotels in four price categories, grouped in the following areas: Dublin city centre, north suburbs, south suburbs and south coast. Although the tourist information offices at Dublin Airport and Suffolk Street have hotel booking facilities, you are advised to book your accommodation well in advance.

Many hotels, mostly in the top of the range, add a service charge to the quoted price, and rates shoot up during special events. Be sure to ask what is included in the quoted rates: ask about VAT (government tax), service and breakfast (after a full Irish breakfast you probably won't need much lunch). Also ask about weekend rates and other special offers or check on the hotel's website.

As a basic guide to room prices, we have used the following symbols for a double room with bath or shower (en suite), usually including breakfast, service charge and tax:

€€€€	over 190 euros
€€€	140–190uros
€€	90–140 euros
€	below 90 euros

CITY CENTRE

The Parliament Hotel € *Lord Edward Street, Dublin 2, tel: 670 8777, www.parliamenthotel.ie.* This smart, good-value hotel sits opposite Dublin Castle and just around the corner from Temple Bar, it also has the lively Legends Bar, featuring Irish music and dancing every night. 63 rooms.

Blooms Hotel € *6 Anglesea Street, Temple Bar, Dublin 2, tel: 671 5622, www.blooms.ie.* A convenient modern hotel in the Temple Bar area,

Blooms is a decent choice for partygoers, but not for those planning a quiet night. Downstairs is Club M. 86 rooms.

Brooks Hotel €€ *Drury Street, Dublin 2, tel: 670 4000*, www.brooks hotel.ie. With a great location just a short walk from Dublin's Grafton Street, Brooks is a smart choice in the centre of the city. Rooms are spacious and comfortable and there are plasma screens and DVD players in the newer rooms. 98 rooms.

Buswells Hotel €€ *23–27 Molesworth Street, Dublin 2, tel: 614 6500*, www.buswells.ie. Centrally located (opposite the National Museum and parliament) in a former Georgian townhouse, Buswells has an old-world atmosphere and period furnishings. Bar popular with politicians. 67 rooms.

Castle Hotel €€ *2–4 Great Denmark Street, Dublin 1, tel: 874 6949*, www.castle-hotel.ie. The Castle Hotel consists of three adjacent and tastefully restored Georgian buildings, close to Parnell Square. Authentically restored décor combined with modern comfort. Small conference facilities and parking. 48 rooms.

Central Hotel €€ *1–5 Exchequer Street, Dublin 2, tel: 679 7302*, www. centralhoteldublin.ie. A modest and comfortable hotel, well-located midway between Temple Bar and Grafton Street, and furnished in Victorian style. First floor Library Bar attracts literary types. 70 rooms.

Clarence Hotel €€€ *6–8 Wellington Quay, Dublin 2, tel: 407 0800*, www.theclarence.ie. Each room is uniquely designed in a contemporary manner in this handsome hotel, built in 1852. Adjacent to Temple Bar and overlooking the River Liffey, it has a lovely interior and a fine restaurant, The Tea Rooms. Parking. 44 rooms, 4 suites and 1 penthouse.

Clarion Hotel €€€ *Liffey Valley, Dublin 22, tel: 625 8000*, www.clarion hotelliffeyvalley.com. Clarion is a good option with contemporary-styled rooms, luxurious suites and serviced apartments for those planning on a longer stay. The hotel also has the Sanovitae Health and Fitness Club with gym and swimming pool. Family packages include a visit to the Tayto Park and Dublin Zoo. 151 rooms and suites, 14 apartments.

Cliff Townhouse €€€ *22 St Stephens Green, Dublin 2, tel: 01-638 3939*, www.clifftownhouse.com. An upmarket guesthouse offering discreet, low-key luxury above a celebrated restaurant and oyster bar, an outpost of the gourmet destination Cliff House Hotel in Ardmore. A wonderful central location in Georgian Dublin and a quiet place for a romantic getaway. Handy for shopping and dining out. 10 rooms.

Conrad Dublin €€€€ *Earlsfort Terrace, Dublin 2, tel: 602 8900*, http://conradhotels1.hilton.com. Situated just off St Stephen's Green, this glass construction opposite the National Concert Hall houses one of Ireland's few five-star hotels. The Conrad's gourmet restaurant, traditional pub and elegant tearoom could make it difficult to leave. 191 rooms and 15 suites.

O'Callaghan Davenport Hotel €€€€ *Merrion Square, Dublin 2, tel: 607 3500*, www.ocallaghanhotels.com. The neoclassical style of the impressive facade of this elegant 1860s building is carried over into its vast atrium lobby. Fine-dining restaurant, bar, conference facilities, car park. 102 rooms and 12 suites.

Dylan €€€€ *Eastmoreland Place, Dublin 2, tel: 660 3000*, www.dylan. ie. A chic and stylish boutique hotel in a quiet location off Baggot Street, about a 15-minute walk from Grafton Street. The individually designed rooms include plasma screens, customised beds and underfloor-heated bathrooms. 41 rooms and suites.

Fitzsimons Hotel €€ *21–22 Wellington Quay, Dublin 2, tel: 677 9315*, www.fitzsimonshotel.com. If you're coming to Dublin to experience a weekend you'll soon forget (i.e. with the lads/lasses) this is the place for you. A huge nightclub and four bars over five floors make it an all-night affair. By day, the Millennium Bridge provides access to the city's best shopping areas. 22 rooms.

Fitzwilliam Hotel €€€€ *St Stephen's Green, Dublin 2, tel: 478 7000*, www.fitzwilliamhotel.com. This modern, upmarket hotel is located on the Green and has a contemporary and understated elegance. There are views of Dublin from the lovely roof garden. Among its three restaurants, the Michelin-starred Thornton's is one of Dublin's finest. 130 rooms.

Grafton Capital €€ *Stephen's Street Lower, Dublin 2, tel: 648 1100*, www.graftoncapitalhotel.com. This is a good three-star townhouse hotel with a great location in the centre of the lively Cultural Quarter near Grafton Street. Across the road, a string of Dublin's best cafés and bars await exploration. 75 rooms.

Gresham Hotel €€€ *23 Upper O'Connell Street, Dublin 1, tel: 874 6881*, www.gresham-hotels.com. One of Dublin's legendary hotels, the Gresham is based in the heart of the city, near the General Post Office. The fine, early 19th-century building, with its marble floors and large rooms offers luxurious accommodation. Two restaurants, two bars. 288 rooms and suites.

Maldron Hotel Smithfield €€ *The Plaza, Smithfield, Dublin 7, tel: 485 0900*, www.maldronhotels.com. There are fine views of the city from the floor-to-ceiling windows in the rooms at the front of this contemporary hotel. The hotel is in the legal district behind the Four Courts, so nights are quiet. Temple Bar is just across the river, O'Connell Street is a short stroll, or you can hop on a red line Luas (tram). 92 rooms.

The Marker Hotel €€€€ *Grand Canal Square, Docklands, Dublin 2, tel: 01-687 5100*, www.themarkerhoteldublin.com. This was the first luxury hotel to open in Dublin since the economic crash: six floors of iconic architecture and interior design situated in the heart of the futuristic new docklands development area. Rooftop lounge, 23m infinity pool, indoor-outdoor brasserie. 187 rooms.

Merrion Hotel €€€€ *Upper Merrion Street, Dublin 2, tel: 603 0600*, www.merrionhotel.com. This elegant five-star hotel was created from four Georgian town houses. Its gracious setting, discreet service and beautifully appointed rooms and suites offer an outstanding experience. One of Dublin's notable restaurants, Patrick Guilbaud (see page 109) is located here. 123 rooms and 19 suites.

Mont Clare Hotel €€ *Merrion Square, Dublin 2, tel: 607 3800*, www.ocallaghanhotels.com. An attractive hotel with a traditional club-like feel, set in a Georgian building on lovely Merrion Square. Convenient for the National Art Gallery, Trinity College and other attractions. Restaurant, bar, car park. 72 rooms and 2 suites.

The Morgan €€€ *10 Fleet Street, Temple Bar, Dublin 2, tel: 643 7000,* www.themorgan.com. The most stylish boutique hotel in Temple Bar. You should stay here if you've come to live it up (or seduce). You can start in the chic cocktail bar, which also serves tapas. 106 rooms.

Morrison Hotel €€€€ *Ormond Quay, Dublin 1, tel: 887 2400,* www.morrisonhotel.ie. One of Dublin's most sophisticated hotels, set in a modern building overlooking the River Liffey. The Morrison Grill is informal, yet elegant, and the intimate new-look Quay 14, an all-day bar-café which overlooks the River Liffey, is a great place for a cocktail. 138 rooms.

Number 31 €€€ *31 Leeson Close, Lower Leeson Street, Dublin 2, tel: 676 5011,* www.number31.ie. This upscale B&B, formerly home to a leading modernist architect, is a favourite with regular visitors to Dublin. It features spacious rooms, listed architecture, a sunken lounge with fireplace, and a fabulous Irish breakfast in the conservatory. 21 rooms.

The Paramount €€ *Parliament Street, Dublin 2; tel: 417 9900,* www.paramounthotel.ie. The Paramount has good rooms and a gentleman's club feel with tobacco-tones and 1930s styling. The location is hard to beat. 64 rooms.

Russell Court Hotel € *21–25 Harcourt Street, Dublin 2, tel: 478 4066,* www.russellcourthotel.ie. Two Georgian houses make up this hotel with its Victorian-style décor, plus a two-storey cottage at the rear of the hotel. Restaurant, nightclub and bars. 42 rooms.

Shelbourne Hotel €€€€ *27 St Stephen's Green, Dublin 2, tel: 663 4500,* www.marriott.com. Dublin's most famous hotel lives up to its five-star rating. Some rooms overlook the Green, and all are furnished for style and comfort. A very good restaurant and two bars; try the lobby for afternoon tea. 265 rooms and 13 suites.

Staunton's on the Green €€ *83 St Stephen's Green South, Dublin 2, tel: 478 2300,* www.stauntonsonthegreen.ie. This exclusive Georgian guesthouse overlooks St Stephen's Green in front and the Iveagh Gardens to the rear. A well-preserved historic building, with splendid high ceilings and windows. The spacious rooms are all en suite. 40 rooms.

Temple Bar Hotel €€ *Fleet Street, Temple Bar, Dublin 2, tel: 612 9200*, www.templebarhotel.com. Pleasant hotel in Temple Bar, near clubs and pubs, and a stone's throw away from Grafton Street. Restaurant and bar. 129 rooms.

Trinity City Hotel €€ *Pearse Street, Dublin 2, tel: 648 1000*, www.trinitycityhotel.com. Formerly Trinity Capital, with atmospheric Victorian décor in the lobby and bar. Bright, contemporary rooms with cherry wood furnishings. Most rooms have internet access; mini-suites have Jacuzzi baths. Restaurant. 195 rooms.

Trinity Lodge €€ *12 South Frederick Street, Dublin 2, tel: 617 0900*, www.trinitylodge.com. Tucked away on a quiet side street near Trinity College, you can't get any more central than this and it's difficult to find a quieter location. Inside, the rooms have light oak furniture and big, comfy beds. Outside you are in one of Dublin's best café society areas. 23 rooms.

The Westbury €€€€ *Grafton Street, Dublin 2, tel: 679 1122*, www.doylecollection.com. A favourite with visiting celebrities, the Westbury is a lush, opulent oasis just off Grafton Street. The Gallery is a favourite for afternoon tea and the Marble Bar is a chic spot to have a cocktail. 205 rooms and suites.

The Westin €€€€ *Westmoreland Street, Dublin 2, tel: 645 1000*, www.thewestindublin.com. The Westin sits in a prime city centre location in a grand historic building, which used to be the Allied Irish Bank. It is everything you'd expect from an international 5-star with luxurious guest rooms, fully-equipped gym and fine dining. 163 rooms and suites.

Wynn's Hotel €€ *35–39 Lower Abbey Street, Dublin 1, tel: 874 5131*, www.wynnshotel.ie. This old-fashioned city centre hotel has been a landmark since Victorian times and is just around the corner from the Abbey Theatre. Still a favourite meeting spot for Dubliners with a genuine local buzz, and a busy restaurant at lunch and early evening. Bar, conference facilities, parking. 65 rooms.

NORTH OF THE CENTRE

Egan's Guesthouse € *7–9 Iona Park, Glasnevin, Dublin 9, tel: 830 3611,* www.eganshouse.com. Red brick guesthouse in a pleasant terrace of Edwardian houses, near the splendid Botanic Gardens, Croke Park and the airport. Car park. 32 rooms.

Regency Hotel €€ *Swords Road, Whitehall, Dublin 9, tel: 837 3544,* www.regencyhotels.com. A handy place to stay if you're coming in too late for the fun, or too early for the sun. Located between the city and the airport, the rooms are modern and the theme restaurant will feed you well. 280 rooms.

SOUTH OF THE CENTRE

Bewley's Hotel Ballsbridge €€ *Merrion Road, Ballsbridge, Dublin 4, tel: 668 1111,* www.bewleyshotels.com. A spacious and modern hotel behind a restored 1793 facade, with comfortable, reasonably priced rooms, sleeping up to two adults and two children on a per room rate. The bar is a popular meeting place, and relatively quiet. Restaurant, parking. 304 rooms.

Double Tree Hilton Dublin - Burlington Road €€ *Upper Leeson Street, Dublin 4, tel: 618 5600,* www.doubletree3.hilton.com. A huge and popular hotel, the Double Tree has Dublin's largest conference facilities. Great rates available online. Restaurants, bars, car park. 500 rooms and 6 suites.

Glenveagh Townhouse € *31 Northumberland Road, Ballsbridge, Dublin 4, tel: 668 4612,* www.glenveagh.com. A pleasant Victorian house a 15-minute walk or short bus ride from centre. Quiet location. Parking. 13 rooms.

Herbert Park Hotel €€ *Anglesea Road, Ballsbridge, Dublin 4, tel: 667 2200,* www.herbertparkhotel.ie. Stylish, comfortable, modern hotel in the Embassy district. The lounge, bar and restaurant feature furnishings by Irish designers. Rooms have king-size beds. Fitness and business facilities, free car park. 150 rooms and 3 suites.

Lansdowne Hotel €€ *27–29 Pembroke Road, Ballsbridge, Dublin 4, tel: 668 2522,* www.lansdownehotel.ie. This is a small, friendly family-run hotel, set back from a tree-lined road in Ballsbridge. Druid's Restaurant, traditional bar, car park. 40 rooms.

Premier Suites Dublin €€€ *Stephen's Hall, 14–17 Lower Leeson Street, Dublin 2, tel: 638 1111,* www.premiersuitesdublin.com. These luxurious serviced apartments are ideal for anyone planning a longer stay. Each suite has a spacious living area with plasma TV, hi-fi and broadband. 27 suites, 3 penthouses.

Raglan Lodge €€ *10 Raglan Road, Ballsbridge, Dublin 4, tel: 660 6697.* In a Victorian house dating from 1861, this hotel offers a quiet stay in a peaceful location near the American Embassy and 10 minutes by bus from Dublin's centre. Award-winning breakfast. Parking. 7 rooms.

Sandymount Hotel €–€€ *Herbert Road, Landsowne Road, Sandymount, Dublin 4, tel: 614 2000,* www.sandymounthotel.ie. A family-run hotel in an extended Victorian building near Lansdowne Road DART, the Aviva Stadium and Sandymount Strand (for walkers and runners). Functional but comfortable en-suite rooms. Children's play area. Restaurant, bar, parking. 180 rooms.

SOUTH COAST

Fitzpatrick Castle Hotel €€–€€€ *Killiney Hill Road, Killiney, Co. Dublin, tel: 230 5400,* www.fitzpatrickcastle.com. This period residence sits in 3.5 hectares (9 acres) of landscaped gardens and wooded grounds, overlooking Dublin Bay. Restaurants, bar, fitness centre, swimming pool and games room; golf, tennis and horse riding available off-site. Car park. 113 rooms and suites.

Rochestown Lodge Hotel and Spa €€ *Rochestown Avenue, Dun Laoghaire, Co. Dublin, tel: 285 3555,* www.rochestownlodge.com. Rooms have contemporary furnishings, many with views of the Wicklow Mountains. Family rooms are available. Facilities include a gym and health centre. 90 rooms and suites.

INDEX

INSIGHT ⊙ GUIDES POCKET GUIDE

DUBLIN

First Edition 2016

Editor: Kate Drynan
Author: Alice Fellows
Head of Production: Rebeka Davies
Picture Editor: Tom Smyth
Cartography Update: Carte
Update Production: AM Services
Photography Credits: Alamy 21; Apa
Publications 32; Kevin Cummins/Apa
Publications 13; Corrie Wingate/Apa
Publications 5M, 6TL, 7TC, 7MC, 7T, 8L, 27,
28, 43, 45, 96, 98, 104; Doug Plummer/Apa
Publications 9, 39, 58, 61, 63, 67, 76, 78;
Dreamstime 4MC; Fáilte Ireland 71; Glyn
Genin/Apa Publications 4TC, 4ML, 4TL, 5TC,
5MC, 5M, 5MC, 6TC, 7M, 8R, 9R, 16, 22, 24,
26, 34, 36, 41, 42, 47, 48, 49, 50, 51, 52, 53,
55, 56, 62, 65, 69, 79, 82, 84, 86, 91, 101, 102;
Ireland Tourist Board 80; iStockphoto 5T, 31;
Nathaniel Gonzales/Apa Publications 6TL;
Nowitz Photography/Apa Publications 7M,
15, 46, 75, 93, 94; Public domain 6ML, 18;
Shutterstock 11; Tourism Ireland 73, 88
Cover Picture: Getty Images

Distribution

UK, Ireland and Europe: Apa Publications
(UK) Ltd; sales@insightguides.com
United States and Canada: Ingram Publisher
Services; ips@ingramcontent.com
Australia and New Zealand: Woodslane;
info@woodslane.com.au
Southeast Asia: Apa Publications (SN) Pte;
singaporeoffice@insightguides.com

Hong Kong, Taiwan and China:
Apa Publications (HK) Ltd;
hongkongoffice@insightguides.com
Worldwide: Apa Publications (UK) Ltd;
sales@insightguides.com

**Special Sales, Content Licensing
and CoPublishing**
Insight Guides can be purchased in bulk
quantities at discounted prices. We can create
special editions, personalised jackets and
corporate imprints tailored to your needs.
sales@insightguides.com;
www.insightguides.biz

Contact us
Every effort has been made to provide
accurate information in this publication,
but changes are inevitable. The publisher
cannot be responsible for any resulting loss,
inconvenience or injury. We would appreciate
it if readers would call our attention to any
errors or outdated information. We also
welcome your suggestions; please contact us
at: hello@insightguides.com
www.insightguides.com

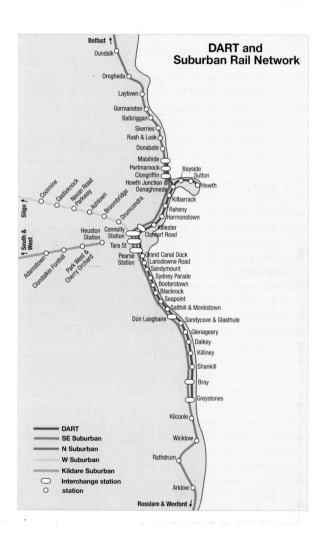